The Forest Soldier

John Roman Nurt

The True Story of
Sergeant "Avalanche,"
Poland's Greatest Partisan Unit
and Their Fight Against Two Evils

The Forest Soldier: The True Story of Sergeant "Avalanche," Poland's Greatest Partisan Unit and Their Fight Against Two Evils
by John Roman Nurt

Copyright © Kathleen Nurt, 2023
All rights reserved.

ISBN: 979-8-9874211-0-9 (hardcover, color)
ISBN: 979-8-9874211-1-6 (hardcover, black and white)
ISBN: 979-8-9874211-2-3 (paperback)

First Edition January 2023

Edited by Larissa Doyle, Kathleen Nurt, Benjamin Knuth, Renata Kraft, and Tracey Davis.
Translations contributed by Danuta Knuth.
Cover illustration by Kenneth Doyle.
Cover design and layout by Isabella Nurt and Larissa Doyle.
Interior layout by David Trawinski of DAMTE Associates.

Polish Eagle motif created from Licensed Adobe Stock Image #47189328 by HP... Photo. Kotwica Polish Home Army "Anchor" symbols used under Creative Commons License Kotwica symbol © Liftarn / Wikimedia Commons / CC-BY-SA-2.5; and Kotwica jako symbol Polski Walczącej by Pawel Kruczyński / CC BY-SA 4.0.

This is a work of narrative nonfiction, augmented by recollected conversations as generationally passed down by members of the Nurt/Niedźwiecki Family. Some parts have been fictionalized in varying degrees, for various purposes.

The opinions expressed in this manuscript are solely the opinions of the author and do not represent the opinions or thoughts of the publisher.

This book may not be reproduced, transmitted, or stored in whole or in part by any means, including graphic, electronic, or mechanical without the express written consent of the publisher except in the case of brief quotations embodied in critical articles and reviews.

Published by Kotwica Press
forest-soldier@kotwica.org

This book is dedicated

to my father,

Józef Niedźwiecki

and my aunt,

Helena Niedźwiecka.

They never got the recognition they deserved.

And to my Uncle Jan,

who gave everything.

Introduction

by Larissa Niedzwiecka Doyle

Two young men are hiding in a thicket at dawn. One is just a teenage boy; the other is a few years older. They are sleep-deprived, sore and battle-weary. The morning light is faint, diffused through the autumn mist and the smoke that still lingers from the prior day's battle.

They know that no matter which way they turn, there's no escape.

One of the two figures, the younger one, drops to his knees and begins to pray, while the other raises a gun, ready to take aim at the kneeling boy's skull.

When someone picks up a book like this, one of the first questions they usually want answered is: *How much of this is true?*

Well, in the case of this book, in the words of the author, "all the most amazing stories are true." The scene described above really happened, and is the lead-up to one of the most incredible moments of the book. The amazing escapes, miraculous strokes of luck, intense battles, brilliant achievements, poignant deaths and intense suffering are all true history.

My brother John wrote this book to tell the World War II story of our father, Uncle, Jan, and Aunt Helena, describing what they experienced in Poland between 1939 and 1945.

Our father, Józef, the main focus of this book, died quite suddenly in 1989. He left behind notes, an outline, and a draft of one chapter of a memoir.

John took on the task of piecing together the story outlined in our father's notes, and spent two decades researching the details. He contacted men who fought alongside our father, interviewing some in person and corresponding with others. He read as many firsthand accounts as he could find. Many of these were translated from Polish by our cousin Danuta, Helena's eldest daughter, as she sat with John in his office surrounded by books and papers.

Slowly, John painstakingly created outlines, timelines, and hundreds of pages of his own notes, drawing upon numerous eyewitness reports, our father's writings, and decades of family reminiscences, especially those of our brother Richard Nurt.

John made the decision to tell this story in narrative form, following the precedent that our father set with his own very short manuscript. He also told me that he didn't want to write a dry history book. Instead, he wanted the narrative to be vivid and to capture the feel of the stories as he remembered our father telling them.

It's a daunting task, writing a narrative history that flows as an engaging story without having been there oneself, and it is probably impossible to piece it all back together again with perfect accuracy. Our father and aunt are gone and many of these incidents don't have any living eyewitness accounts to draw from any more.

Due to the secondary-source nature of this work, and the decision to tell the story as a narrative, there are parts of the book that fall under the scope of "artistic license." This includes almost all dialog and the names of a few peripheral characters, all of which are noted in the appendix at the end of the book. Also, the descriptive details of certain battles and scenes are based on how John visualized them as he listened to our father's stories, or as he heard or read the accounts of other eyewitnesses.

That said, throughout the book John's intent was to honor the truth of who these people were, as well as the historical accuracy of the story to the best of his ability.

In most cases, the dialogue reflects stories real eyewitnesses told, paraphrased to align as closely as memory allows. For example, much of the dialogue between Józef and his brother Jan was based on stories our father told many times.

Although we don't know what our father was thinking throughout the war, we can make an educated guess based on our knowledge of who he was as a person, the kinds of things he said and did in later life, and the thoughts he committed to paper in his own unfinished memoir.

Our aunt Helena, the only family member who immigrated with our father to the United States, lived much longer than Józef, but only spoke of the war with extreme difficulty.

When I was a freshman in college I interviewed Helena for a history class assignment. The interview was shocking to me. I was only fourteen when our father died, and I hadn't heard many of his war stories. Even though I spent a lot of time near my aunt, she rarely ever mentioned the war. So while I knew that she had survived Ravensbruck concentration camp, it was an abstract knowledge, lacking in detail.

Helena was an incredibly vibrant person. She was cheerful and self-possessed, with a great sense of humor and a larger-than-life personality. When she laughed, everyone around would laugh with her. She had a trademark whistle that could instantly summon grandchildren from play or turn their heads in the middle of a soccer match. Her intelligence was as piercing as her whistle: she spoke English and Russian fluently and understood German quite well, in addition to her native Polish.

The thing that made a deep impression on me when I interviewed Helena was the way this confident woman fell apart when trying to relay her experiences of the war. As she spoke, she shook violently from embodied trauma. Her language became broken, halting, and her voice was choked. Her attempts to tell her story jumped around in chaotic vignettes, untethered to chronology as her psyche seemed to disintegrate in front of me. I felt terrible for asking her to remember.

There is no doubt that Helena, our father, and their entire family experienced profound darkness and witnessed great evil. There are countless books that dwell on the horrors of World War II in vivid detail. This is not one of those books. John chose not to focus on the darkest aspects of the history, but rather on the stories that were most recounted in the family. Neither our father nor his sister wanted to dwell on the nightmarish atrocities in front of their children or grandchildren.

Nor is this book an academic work of history. While it fills in some gaps in history, from an arena of the war largely unknown due to Soviet repression and falsifications of the records by both Soviets and Nazis, it is nonetheless not a primary source. This book is part of a pantheon of stories that could not be told as long as the Communists were still in power in Poland.

For sweeping firsthand accounts written by direct participants, it is recommended to consult the books that served as John's main sources in putting together the timeline and overview of this narrative. They are listed in a bibliography at the end of this book.

John wrote this book because our father, aunt, and uncle never got the recognition they deserved for their achievements, sacrifices and intrepid actions. He wrote it to tell an exceptional adventure story full of bravery, luck, suffering, perseverance, betrayal, and even miracles. And he wrote it for our family, because he wants us to know that our parents' and grandparents' legacy should be a reminder that we can, in John's words, "survive suffering or any type of difficulties, and keep going." As he put it, "Amazing things can happen, if you just keep the faith, keep fighting, and keep your integrity."

Prologue

JERRY WALKED OUT To the area of the garden he wanted to work on. There was always something productive to do around the house and the forty acres. It was too early for planting, so some general cleanup was the modest goal. Then maybe a walk around the pond and a bit into the woods before going in. Paulina would make him something to eat. He was over seventy years old and most days went something like this, with the type of work dependent on the seasonal rhythms and whatever needed fixing on the house. It was perhaps the most peaceful and pleasant time of his life. In the evening he would watch the news and read the paper for updates about Poland. The Solidarity Movement was convulsing the country, and all of Eastern Europe, too. It was a proud but nervous time for Polish-Americans.

After just a few moments raking, he felt that something was wrong. A hint of dizziness rolled through him and a pulling sensation affected his whole right side. He headed back towards the house. The rake slipped from his hand to the ground, surprising him. Momentarily puzzled by the loss of grip strength, he leaned slightly to pick it up, but then turned away and limped more urgently up the slight hill to the porch entrance. Once in through the door he called out to his wife Paulina, "Lulu...I think I am having a stroke."

At the hospital, the diagnosis was confirmed. His speech was difficult and slurred. He spoke on the phone to each of his four children, and each conversation ended with, "I love you, Dad."

In fact, for the past year or two, as if by a secret cue that time is not limitless, his two sons and two daughters ended every conversation with a heartfelt, "I love you." Nothing had prompted that change then, but Jerry had noticed, and mentioned to Paulina how much he appreciated it. The kids were all living out of town, but would be coming home. He hoped to improve quickly, so that they could visit him at the house and not the hospital.

He built the house with his own hands and a small crew. It was a chalet style home with steep roof lines and a tall windowed peak. The property lay mostly to the home's south and was extensively wooded. Beautifully steep-sided Hemlock shaded ravines cut through the forest, with a babbling little brook flowing through them. Maples, Ash, and Beech trees were prominent in this part of New York State, but Jerry knew all the rarer trees also, like the Basswood, Cucumber, and Tulip trees. He loved the woods. He always had.

In the harsh artificial lights of the hospital, Jerry worried that his ability to walk the woods would be lost. Once he got home, he could still work on his memoirs, though. So far, he had two outlines organized that laid out the whole war experience. That last night and day in Kampinos, though, that story was already written out. The happenings of that night were still so vivid - vivid, yet still hard to believe - so he completed this chapter first. It was a miracle - yes, an actual miracle - that both saved and changed his life.

He had lived such a quiet, modest existence after the war, changing his name from Józef Niedźwiecki to Jerome "Jerry" Nurt to avoid any possibility of problems with the Soviets. No one knew his record. Fellow soldiers said he was "very famous" back in his home region, a region that he could never hope to return to as long as it was controlled by the communists.

Lieutenant Niedźwiecki had been awarded four Medals of Valor, the maximum that could be achieved for heroism in battle. The medal of the silver cross of merit with swords was awarded also, for "non-combat actions in perilous circumstances."

Most impressively, he was awarded the Virtuti Militari (Medal of Virtue), Poland's highest honor, equivalent to the American Medal of Honor. He had led a squadron of one hundred cavalry soldiers on horseback, all while in occupied territory. He was shot two different times but continued fighting, and then was injured by a bomb blast. He fought or was involved in underground activity for the whole war, from 1939 to 1945, initially under the pseudonym *"Szary" - Gray*, and later as *"Lawina" - Avalanche*.

He thought back to those years when two evil behemoths wrestled over Poland, grappling and trading blows, and crushing so many innocents beneath their feet. He remembered the NKVD prison and afterwards the cruel and murderous Nazi occupation. He remembered his brother Jan and the Iwieniec Uprising. He thought about the night raids, and the snow caves, and the crossing of the Vistula. There was the betrayal, and the secret order, and being surrounded by five thousand German troops. How did he survive?

Jerry would never make it back home from the hospital. There would be another major stroke. He wouldn't walk the woods again or finish his memoirs. The outlines and notes would sit in a box for many years. In that box, and in the many other histories published after communism was defeated in Poland, were incredible stories of perhaps the greatest partisan unit of World War II.

THIS IS HIS WAR STORY.
THE STORY OF LIEUTENANT NIEDŹWIECKI,
SERGEANT AVALANCHE,
THE FOREST SOLDIER.

Chapter One

Lwów

JÓZEF NIEDŹWIECKI SAT LEANING against the wall of a pockmarked brick building on a rubble strewn street in the city of Lwów. It was mid-September 1939 and he was trying to fully comprehend what had just happened to him over the last two weeks, and moreover, what had happened to his beloved Poland.

Józef had been so confident in Poland's ability to fight off the German attack. Everyone had been. Hearing the news of the decision to capitulate was a visceral shock. Things had gone horribly awry right from the start, and then got worse. The Germans had unveiled their new "lightning war" to devastating effect, punching through the Polish lines and throwing the whole defense plan into chaos. Communications and supply lines were immediately smashed, and only a massive retreat and reorganization could have saved the Polish Army. But what happened next was unthinkable. At the worst moment possible, Poland was invaded from the undefended east by the Soviet Union.

Defeated by treachery was how Józef explained it to himself.

The first week of the war Józef had fought in some skirmishes near the southern border, and then ended up defending Lwów from the surrounding Nazi seige. General Langner had done a remarkable job organizing random units into a strong defense. The Germans couldn't break it. The Poles were willing to fight to the last man. Morale was strong when the confusing news about Russia filtered in. The order to give up the fight was met with universal anguish. Germany ceded the city to their Russian partners and no one knew what would happen next.

The march from the border to Lwów had been an ordeal. Germany had indiscriminately attacked civilian towns and villages, especially by air. Józef had seen the heartbreaking destruction with each mile. Buildings were burned out or blasted apart. There were dead livestock everywhere. Horses lay stinking and bloated along roadways, their legs jutting out at hideous angles. The faces of mothers and children he encountered looked alternately stupefied with shock or contorted with suffering. Every hour had brought new tragedies and outrages. He steeled himself against despair by promising revenge against the invaders. He would fight. That he knew for sure. *They would pay for this!*

So here he sat, grimy, sweaty, and exhausted, waiting for orders. He spotted one of his fellow unit members from the Borderland Defense Corps, or *Korpus Ochrony Pogranicza* (KOP) in Polish.

Józef yelled out to him, "Any news?"

Bohdan strolled over and replied, "The Russians want all officers to gather up and report in. They are promising not to arrest anyone. You should head over to the courtyard and meet with the others."

"What about you?" Józef asked Bohdan, who unlike himself was not an officer.

"I am free to leave, it seems, so I am heading home."

"Better get going before they change their mind. Good luck to you."

Józef pulled himself up, shook hands with his friend, then began walking decidedly in the opposite direction of the Soviet authorities. He turned a corner, and collided into three Red Army soldiers, who immediately disarmed Józef and marched him back. With every step a sense of foreboding increased. Despite being only twenty years old, Józef's early start in the KOP had brought him to the rank of corporal. He was proud of his rank, though it didn't occur to him that then, at that fateful moment, it was a liability.

As he joined the mass of fellow officers, he began to survey the surroundings. Those first inclinations of impending danger seemed to be borne out. Stern looking Russian soldiers watched over the Polish men with their rifles at the ready. The Soviet officers grimly entered names and directed the Polish officers to a makeshift barracks to wait. The process took many hours and it didn't make sense. Why were they being held?

More guards seemed to be arriving. For what purpose? Józef had his name documented and then spent the night on the floor of the overcrowded holding area.

That very afternoon the promise was broken, and the news spread like an electrical current through the officer ranks. They were all under arrest and would be held until further notice. The officers were transported to the nearby city of Tarnopol, and then after a long wait at the train depot, Józef's turn came to be ordered into a crowded boxcar.

Chapter Two

First Escape

JÓZEF NIEDŹWIECKI HAD BEEN TRAVELING by train for almost a full day when he finalized his determination to try to escape. He absolutely could not bear this journey into some unknown fate any longer. Growing up near the Soviet border had impressed upon him a clear fear of Russian motives, which only added to the general distrust all Poles held for their neighbor. The invasion sealed the deal. While those around him seemed resigned to let this imprisonment play out, he knew now that he could not continue waiting. Every fiber of his being was urging action. But where and how? He actively began scouting the situation. The train was clattering along at a fast clip. Long stretches of countryside were passing by with occasional towns. They weren't stopping. He could wait for a stop when they were disembarked and try to run, but what if they stopped at some enclosed prison camp? The sooner he could escape the better too, before they went too far into Russia.

A Soviet soldier stood guard at each end of the car. Some of the Polish men had been told in Tarnopol that they would be released when the train passed near their home region, but the train continued its eastward journey with no signs of changing course. Murmuring and tension grew with each hour. A confrontation began as some of the prisoners started yelling at the guards.

The angry men gathered around them, pressing ever closer. The Russian at the front of the car yelled at them to step back and tried to raise his rifle, but several hands gripped the rifle immediately and wrestled it back down. More prisoners joined in and tried ripping the rifle away as the guard shouted for help.

"Where are we going?" rang out from around the car. Two more guards showed up outside the forward door and tried to get in, but were thwarted as the crowding men held the door partially shut. A shot rang out from the back as the struggle for the rifles continued. The rear guard disappeared completely in the melee and the back door suddenly flew open.

Józef joined several men who rushed to escape. The first man paused at the open door as there was nowhere to go except the next car or the fast moving ground below. He looked around and then started climbing up the back wall of the car. The second and third man followed and then Józef went up, gripping the cross pieces of wooden framing as a ladder. Once upon the top of the car he reached back to help several more men escape to the roof.

The procession stopped. Did the guards regain control or was this just all who dared make the climb? The men crouched on the roof in the wind and rocking of the fast moving train.

Now what? he thought. *Perhaps this was an impulsive and foolhardy move?*

They looked all around and tried to gauge the possibility of jumping, but at this height and speed the odds of injury or death were too great. One of the men pointed far ahead down the tracks. They all saw the wide ribbon of water ahead where the train would cross a river. It was their chance, and they quickly lined up, crouching along the edge of the roof, preparing to jump. They would have to clear the steel guardrails along the bridge and hope that the landing zone was free of rocks or logs. Continuing to ride the roof was out of the question. They had to jump.

The train approached the river quickly, mechanically devouring the track with its metallic clanking. It looked wide enough to avoid missing the water and hitting the other shore, but they could not afford to hesitate. Fear gripped Józef, and his fast pounding heart kept time with the beating roar of the train. He pictured slipping and crashing into the guardrails, then rolling under the train wheels. The moment was arriving. He prepared his stance, one foot slightly ahead of the other, one hand on the roof edge ahead, the other prepared to swing out like a long jumper.

A Russian guard appeared, his head and arms rising above the roof edge to see what the escapees were up to, but the nearest Polish soldier kicked at him hard with his boot heel, and the Russian dropped back out of sight.

The river edge came quickly now, and when it passed beneath his feet Józef leaped. Then he was flying through the air, moving forward from the train momentum and outward. He had the brief sensation of slowing down before suddenly speeding downward, watching the water rise to meet him. He hit feet first, went under completely, and felt his boots touch the mud below. He pushed off, rocketing himself back to the surface. He treaded water for a moment and watched the train clatter down the tracks until the last car passed and continued out of sight. He came back to his senses and realized the other men were splashing their way to the nearest shore. After a short swim he felt bottom again and waded in.

Everything had happened so fast he almost could not believe he was free. The men, eight of them had made the escape, sat down together several yards from the river's edge. It took several minutes before the first words were spoken, shocked as they were by the unlikely and heart pounding escape. They rested for a bit, introduced themselves, and then began discussing their task of heading home through the many miles of enemy territory.

They would follow the train tracks back westward, keeping a distance away and avoiding settlements and towns. Eventually they would divide up and head towards their various regions of Poland.

Józef took stock of his situation. He wasn't sure where he was. He had no weapon and no supplies. Luckily he had one advantage. Before his military training he had been a boy scout. He had also grown up in the region of the Naliboki wilderness, where he hunted, fished and trapped game with his brothers from early childhood.

He felt a surge of confidence and optimism as he began walking west with the others. He would make it home for sure, but what would he find there? That was a huge worry. Buoyed by the exhilaration of the escape, they set a fast pace, but hid from any human contact.

In two days they had crossed back into Poland. It would be easier to get some help now, he knew, glad to be in his homeland. However, Poland was now occupied by two hostile powers so they still had to use extreme caution.

After the third day of walking the group split up. Three of them traveled together for two more days until their homeward journey called them to different paths. Alone now, Józef was able to stay the night with a Polish farm family that took him in for a night's rest and some good food. They discussed the war and the confusion over what would happen next. The couple had three boys in the war and none had returned home yet. Before Józef left, they gave him a change of clothes. It was too dangerous to stay in uniform. Much to his surprise, they offered him one of their horses, with the understanding that someday in the future, God willing, he would return it or pay them back. It was an act of great generosity. Perhaps the couple were hoping someone would be so kind if their own missing sons were in need.

Setting out again, he was able to ride the roads now at a fast pace. He circled around the towns, avoiding the Russian soldiers, and slept in the woods. Surviving many tense days and nights, he finally saw signs that he was nearing his hometown, Iwieniec.

The prisoner train from which he had escaped, one of many just like it, continued on its grim journey to the Smolensk region of Russia. There the twenty-two thousand officers and other prominent members of Polish society arrested by the Soviets were interned over the winter.

In April and May of 1940 the prisoners were systematically taken in small groups to the forest areas around Katyń. The NKVD tied the prisoners' hands with barbed wire before executing them all by a gunshot to the back of the neck. The bodies were dumped in excavated pits and bulldozed over to hide the crime. The fate of the men remained unknown until the German army discovered the mass graves in 1943. Only then would Józef realize this was the fate he had so narrowly escaped.

Chapter Three

SOVIET OCCUPATION

IWIENIEC WAS A POLISH TOWN of around five thousand inhabitants, roughly sixty kilometers east of Minsk. On its western edge it bordered the vast Naliboki wilderness. Its small houses, fenced gardens, and colorful barns nestled into a hilly terrain of narrow streets. The skyline was dominated by two Catholic churches, the "white church" of Saint Michael, so called because of its pure white plaster and stone, and the "red church" of Saint Alexis, made of red brick. The Wolma River flowed gently through the city, widening into a placid pool that gave the appearance of a small lake.

The youth of Iwieniec and nearby towns grew up infused with patriotism and faith, as lived and promoted by families, teachers, and clergy. Visitors and new arrivals to the area found the locals to be polite and well mannered. Relations were generally quite good between the city's population of Poles, Belarussians, and Jews. The eastern borderlands were known as the *"Kresy,"* an area of wildernesses, legends, poets and heroes. The locals had a slightly softer and more melodious accent than greater Poland, and had distinct traditions of food and music.

As Józef approached familiar places, memories and emotions flooded over him. The totality of what he had experienced since his unit was called up rolled through his mind. He had been so focused on the fighting and survival that he hadn't had time to reflect on how lucky he was to be alive. He was a different person, arriving home, then when he had left. If he had any vestiges of carefree boyhood a month ago, that innocence seemed suddenly left behind. The red Soviet banners flying from the buildings confirmed that other things had also changed.

He passed the flat meadow where all his childhood friends had held their "Olympics". They had races, javelin throws, and other contests, awarding one another simple prizes like an apple or a carrot. He had been an organizer of the games, so didn't worry too much about winning. Second place was a good goal, lest it look like he set up a contest for his own glory. His little brother Jan though, liked to win and did so often. He was a natural athlete. In addition to physical talents, the seventeen year old Jan was already a legendary practical joker. Just up ahead, Józef could see the widened, pond-like area of the Wolma River, where Jan had once taken two well dressed girls out for a rowboat ride during a wedding reception, then purposely overturned the boat, dunking all three occupants.

The Niedźwiecki home wıoas at the outskirts of town. Józef decided to avoid the main roads and circled around before walking his horse into the backyard of his house. He was home. Immediately family members spotted him and ran out to hug him and cry. His father, brother Jan, and his little sister Helena were first. After a long embrace, Helena went outside, placed two fingers between her lips and blasted out two incredibly loud whistles. This was an almost legendary ability she had, as one could scarcely believe that this petite female frame could produce such a sound. Very quickly his two older sisters, Rufina and Anna, having heard the whistle from blocks away, arrived to investigate the cause, and saw their missing little brother. The emotional reunion continued.

After several days sleeping and eating in his own home, Józef felt recovered enough to begin planning out his precarious future under Soviet occupation. He was in danger, he learned, as the NKVD was looking for former soldiers, especially officers. Prominent members of the town were disappearing, taken in the middle of the night to who knows where. There were spies watching the townspeople, and it was, by then, clear that even before the invasion, these spies had been surveying Iwieniec for future targets.

Helena saw him deep in thought one afternoon and asked him, "So what are you going to do now?"

Although she was only fourteen and still a young girl, Józef looked at her with a newly developed respect. He didn't think of her as a child any longer. With their mother long passed away, Helena had taken on so many of the chores that keep a home. She was hard working and responsible.

Like Józef, the serious times had propelled Helena into an early maturity. He knew that she worried a lot, not an unreasonable reaction to their whole world being turned upside down. He answered her directly and honestly.

"There is a conspiracy forming. An underground group. A few of us are meeting and planning it out. But don't breathe a word of this to anyone."

She nodded to him as if this was a normal and expected thing for him to say. In some ways, it was. Poland had been routinely invaded for hundreds of years. Conspiracy and resistance was in their blood.

Józef knew he could trust her. The three youngest siblings, himself, Jan and Helena were bound together by the shared loss of their mother, and had clung together tightly ever since.

While Józef was risking life planning the eventual overthrow of the Russians, Jan was spending his time playing phonograph records and practicing his dancing.

One day Józef was rounding the corner heading home, when he spotted Helena crouched outside under their front window, which was wide open. Her round face was so near bursting with laughter that her eyes were like slits as she waved him over, motioning to stay down low. He got down in front of her as she pointed inside. As usual the waltzes and mazurkas were blaring out from the phonograph and Jan was gliding vigorously around the front room. He had a broomstick in his hands as a dancing partner.

"Listen," Helena whispered.

Above the music, Jan was talking out loud to his dancing partner, and Helena was suppressing her laughter.

"You keep your back so straight!" Jan exclaimed to the broom. Right away, a seed of suspicion formed in Józef's mind.

"You are a wonderful dancer," Jan continued. A bit over the top, even for him. The notes continued to flow as Jan glided around the room continuing his commentary. "But with your straw-like hair, and your skinny body, you are much more suitable for my brother than for me."

Józef saw his own widened eyes and open mouth mirrored in Helena's stunned face as they both had the simultaneous moment of realization. The joke was on them… again!

Józef leaped through the open window and tackled his brother in a flash. Helena ran around and in through the door a second later. She picked up the dancing partner and began smacking the wrestling and tumbling boys with hard swings.

"You idiots! You'll smash up the house." She was laughing. Jan was laughing. Józef was laughing. After a minute they separated, red faced and out of breath. The two boys lay flat on their backs, intermittently gasping and chuckling. Helena too, sat down on the floor, tears of laughter flowing down her face. It took several minutes more for them all to recover enough to speak normally.

Later that day, Jan told Józef he planned to come to the next secret meeting of the underground and join up. It was time.

The conspiracy carried on that winter and into spring. They moved meeting locations but most often met at farms or estates out in the country, far away from possible spies. The men took different routes in and arrived separately.

Józef found out that he was already held in high regard. His military experience and the story of his escape had made the rounds, so he was expected to be among the leaders of the new underground group. Their initial goals were to understand all the Soviet power structures in the town and identify the people in charge. They tried to understand the methods and objectives of the enemy. They also began making contact with other groups, which were forming all over the area, to coordinate and exchange information.

One item on the agenda was what to do about Szabunia.

The man named Szabunia was first noticed around Iwieniec in August of 1939, as far as anyone could say. He was a stranger who kept mostly to himself. After the invasion he suddenly became prominent in the Soviet leadership. Turns out he had been spying on the town ahead of time. He immediately denounced many "enemies of the state" who were quickly arrested and taken away. These enemies were normal people in positions of authority or of prominence. So the political leaders, judges, policemen and even just wealthier residents began disappearing from Iwieniec and other nearby towns.

The method was always the same. In the middle of the night the NKVD would show up at a home with soldiers and barking dogs. The families, roused from sleep, were told to pack and be ready to leave in twenty minutes. They were loaded on wagons and taken to the train station. From there they were packed into cattle cars headed for distant locales, often to frigid Siberia. Many died on the cold journey. The victims arrived at gulags and were used as slave labor under horrific conditions.

Quickly Szabunia became well known as the most hated and feared man in the area. He enlisted the help of the town's Jewish and Belarussian residents, under threat, to help identify members of Polish youth organizations. These members were then arrested. This was the beginning of the terrible communist tactic of sowing discord between ethnic groups, who had previously existed well together in Iwieniec for generations. Those who didn't disappear outright were sometimes tortured in the Iwieniec prison to gather even more names and victims. The most galling thing about Szabunia was the way he openly walked about town, and even rode a bicycle between Iwieniec and Naliboki. Blatantly proud and confident in his power and stature, he had no fear.

Iwieniec and Naliboki quickly became just like Soviet towns. Loudspeakers were put up all around the city, and the constant blaring of Russian patriotic music and propaganda added to the tension. The schools were all closed and then reopened as Russian schools. Helena finished up her education in a Russian school learning the Russian language. Business and commerce collapsed. All firearms were confiscated, so hunting game was lost as an option to supplement dwindling food supplies. And worst of all, an oppressive fear descended on the populace as anyone could be the next to face arrest, torture, and exile to Siberia. Even one of the local priests, Father Bajko, had to go into hiding after Szabunia found out he had helped people escape from their imminent arrest.

The underground began discussing plans to eliminate Szabunia, when word filtered out in May that he had disappeared, and the authorities had no idea where he was. A few weeks later Szabunia's body was discovered, badly beaten and quite stiff, hidden under some brush, a short distance off the road he had so brazenly traveled. His hated bicycle lay alongside the body, also mangled beyond repair.

The next meeting of the underground was larger than usual. Arriving at various times for safety, it took several hours for everyone to gather. They took up this waiting time sharing their experiences under occupation and with other general smalltalk. A discussion ensued about the recent news that it was the Grygorcewicz brothers who had administered justice to Szabunia. Mr. Grygorcewicz had been flogged almost to death by Szabunia's henchmen before he and his wife were shipped off to Siberia. Their two grown sons had just happened to be away at the time of arrest and had gone into hiding. They vowed revenge and laid in wait, hidden along the road to Naliboki until the moment that Szabunia pedaled by. The two big strong boys showed him no mercy, just as he had shown none to others. Then they left the region completely, never to be heard from again. Szabunia's reign of terror was over but unfortunately, the NKVD had no shortage of torturers and killers to take his place.

"Did you hear Szabunia was buried in the Catholic cemetery?" asked one of the gathered men.

"No! That's an outrage!" someone stated.

"Terrible, we should dig him up!"

"Shameful! I hope there isn't a cross or a headstone!"

"Funny you ask," interjected Jan out of the blue, "because as it turns out, my brother and I saw his gravesite, and there is a monument."

"What the hell!" and worse exclamations erupted from the crowd.

"Let me tell you all about it," said Jan, standing up and taking the floor.

"You see, my brother and I heard he was buried there, and we couldn't believe it, so we decided to ride over and see for ourselves. We headed down the road and turned left, and right away, wouldn't you know, a girl I know, Basia, sees me and shouts out for me to stop and come in. Now food of course is hard to part with lately, but she always liked me, like most girls, and she offered us some nice pierogi just off the stove, so we stopped and had a meal. Hardly had we started again when another girl called out. This time, Amelia, and she is very pretty, even though a little plump, but that just shows she has some gumption, because these are skinny times of course."

Józef looked around at the crowd of men, who were listening but confused about this story. None of this had actually really happened, so Józef just thought to himself, *Here we go,* and sat back for the show. Obviously Jan had rehearsed this. Among brothers, there is always competition. Best rider, best rifle shot, best dancer, and, of course, even best joke teller was counted in an ongoing, never-ending tabulation. Jan was playing to win a round.

He continued, "Amelia tells us that she is reheating some bigos that she made yesterday, just this very minute, and wouldn't we come in and have a little? So we do, and then we leave, eager to make some tracks, when can you believe it, Maria, one of my very first girlfriends, walks around the corner with a big basket of sausages, and she was right in front of her house, so we could not refuse her, since we have not had a sausage in weeks. Now, you notice that no girls were calling for my brother, probably because he is shorter and not as good looking, and already past his prime. He ate his share though, but not as much as me, so when we rode off again he was fine, but I was a little too full."

By then the men in the room were pretty sure what was going on, but kept quiet, fully invested, some already smiling, awaiting the payoff. Jan went on, gesticulating and acting out his story.

"Riding on a horse with such a full stomach is never recommended, and for me the discomfort started right away. The road is rough there and my horse is a smooth runner, but a bit awkward at slower gaits, so misery overcame me. I felt sick and ready to burst. My stomach was shaking and quivering like a scared rabbit. We couldn't get there soon enough. Just then, when my suffering was at its apex, and I couldn't bear it another minute, we arrived at the cemetery and found the grave. I slowly slid off my horse and looked around for relief. Then, looking at the gravesite, it occurred to me, why not kill two birds with one stone? So I quickly dropped my trousers, and deposited a large and most fitting monument to Szabunia the torturer."

For a half second there was silence, then a huge roar of laughter erupted along with table pounding and foot stomping. The grinning, laughing men took turns slapping Jan on the back and shaking his hand. Amidst the commotion, Jan made eye contact with his brother, tilted his head slightly, and gave him a self-satisfied smile.

The truth was that yes, they had taken a ride to look at the gravesite, and some unknown person had actually left a digested so-called "monument" on it, but that was it as far as their whole experience.

The meeting got down to real business shortly after, and went for two hours before breaking up. Groups of two and three began leaving. It was Jan's last big joke before the calamity that lay ahead.

Chapter Four

CAPTURE AND PRISON

A COUPLE WEEKS LATER Józef and Jan headed out for another clandestine meeting. It was on a woodsy back road, in the autumn of 1940, when their worst fears were realized. As they rode along a lone rider appeared on the crest of a hill heading their way. He wore a Russian uniform, which caused the brothers immediate alarm. As he rode towards them, more riders crested the hill behind him and quickly closed the gap. Instinctively, Józef looked behind for a possible escape, only to see more riders, who spurred their horses into a fast trot. When Józef turned back, the first group had their weapons up and at the ready. The boys were quickly surrounded.

Józef's heart sank as the total surprise left no chance for fight or flight. The armed men dismounted and grabbed the reins from Józef and Jan.

The brothers were ordered off their horses and told to kneel with hands behind their heads. Then a steel enclosed truck arrived. It was obviously a pre-planned action. Józef guessed that they had been under surveillance, and that the NKVD had been tipped off, something he found out later to be the case.

They were shoved into the truck and driven off without delay. The brothers locked eyes for a moment as they bounced along the dusty roads. Death was expected. Suffering and death. So despondent and shocked were they that not a word could be formed in their mind much less actually spoken aloud. After first being imprisoned in Stołpce, they were later moved east.

It was only when they arrived at the NKVD prison in Minsk and were being pushed along down the first corridor that Józef blurted out to his little brother ahead of him, "Be strong!"

They were thrown into separate cells. The stone block rooms were dank, dark and clammy. Heavy steel bars were at the hallway entrance and one small window sat well above head height. An open container, called a *'parasha'*, sat in the corner for human waste, causing a terrible stench. There were dozens of other prisoners in Józef's small cell.

For the first day Józef made small, careful conversations to acquaint himself with his fellow inmates. As far as he could gather, he was the only real underground member, although he kept his background to himself. Other prisoners had been arrested due to the random vagaries of Soviet oppression. They were not criminals, but to the communists your professional status could be criminal, as could your political persuasion, or even your known friendships.

On the second day three new prisoners arrived, but two were taken out for interrogation and never returned. Then the guards came for Józef.

He was marched to an office by the two large men and placed in a wood chair in front of a desk. An NKVD officer stepped in and sat down across from him.

"Good afternoon, Niedźwiecki," said the officer, a man around forty years old, with a soft, fat face and glasses. "I am Kuznetsov, let's begin."

The interrogation commenced in an unthreatening manner. Questions were asked about his service at the front, but then pivoted to questions about the underground. It didn't get very far because Józef gave only the most vague and simplistic replies, punctuated with soft denials and feigned innocence.

After an hour the officer finally said, in a very relaxed and routine way, "I had hoped for a better start. We will continue this later." Then he stood up and left the room.

The two guards returned. For a moment Józef thought he had a reprieve and would head back to the cell. He caught sight of the wooden club just before it blurred into his head and lightning bolts of pain exploded. Then it was a flurry of blows as the two guards swung away with speed and power. Their strikes hit Józef everywhere on his upper body. He was next aware of being on the floor, writhing as the continued clubs hit his ribs, legs, and arms. Instinctively he tried to curl up and roll from the most direct blows, but it was useless in the unrelenting assault. Then it finally stopped.

The two panting guards rested. One lifted the fallen chair upright and sat down. They showed no interest or concern to the limp man on the floor, but made some small talk to each other in Russian. Finally, having rested enough, they stood up. In a haze of pain, Józef felt them start lifting him up to stand. With one guard on each arm, he stumbled and shuffled the agonizing path down the corridor back to the cell, where he was pushed in, only to collapse by the wall. His next thought before passing out was, *Oh no, what about poor Jan?*

The next day nothing happened. He was left alone. Giant welts and bruises covered much of his body. Every movement brought intense pain.

The prisoners were served two tiny food portions in the cell each day: a small lump of black bread and a cup of thin soup. They were escorted to a bathroom once per day, with only the foul bucket for the rest of the day. Józef watched through the blur of his less swollen eye as other prisoners were also returned in a limp and bloody state after interrogation. The following night he was abruptly awoken from sleep at around three am.

"Niedźwiecki! It's your turn!" came the harsh order, and he was again shoved down the hall to the office.

A seated Kuznetsov was joined by a younger agent who stood near his back shoulder. He wore the NKVD cap neatly and stood ramrod straight.

"I am Vasily," he said, as Józef blinked in the harsh lights. "You need to understand that we know a lot about you. It would be very good if we can work together. The Soviet Union can use fine young men like yourself and your brother in the struggle."

So started a two hour round of questions, mostly by Vasily with interjections by the older officer. It was obvious the first objective was to get any and all information on the Polish underground, its members and its activities, before embarking on the *"working together"* phase.

József tried to walk a careful path of giving zero information while pretending he was in some way open to such a flagrant ruse. His goal was to stay alive, keep Jan alive, and avoid the beatings if possible. The session ended with no violence and no information gathered.

Beatings did not disappear from the interrogation menu however, and as the weeks went on, the routine continued. Other prisoners came and went. The cold winter set in and conditions in the cell worsened. The relentless, routine, middle of the night questioning, along with the random beatings took a heavy toll. Despair set in, but they were keeping him alive, thought József, *so do your best to keep it that way. Keep going.*

The nagging urge to just give up and give in was always there. To tell them anything and everything just to end the cycle of suffering tempted him in weak moments. Vasily reiterated at each interrogation that Jan had already confessed everything and exposed all their contacts. It was just József holding out, needlessly prolonging the prison stay.
The claim against Jan was demoralizing. They could be released to begin an eight year gulag sentence with compliance. But József held out. He worried constantly about Jan. *Was he even still alive?*

The determination to hold out was multi-faceted. To give out information would be a betrayal to their underground companions and to Poland itself. They also instinctively understood that once they talked, any incentive for the NKVD to keep them alive would be instantly over. The boys wanted not only to stay alive, but to stay alive with their reputations and self-worth still intact also.

They had spent months in prison when a breakthrough came. A fellow prisoner relayed the news, as he was moved into József's cell, that he had been in a room with Jan for the last few weeks. He described how Jan had received similar interrogation, but perhaps had suffered worse and more frequent beatings. Apparently, Jan couldn't resist subtly mocking the two guards, taking advantage of their stupidity with jokes and vague insults until even their dull brains caught on.

The prisoners had coined nicknames for the two thugs. Sergei was a large round shouldered man with a pallid yellow complexion and bulging eyes. He had thin light brown whiskers that matched his close cropped hair. He was dubbed as "the Carp" or sometimes for variety just "Fish."

The second guard, Pavel, was a huge man with a huge head, dominated by a low forehead and long mouth. His skin was bumpy and unpleasant. He was dubbed "Toad."

The nicknames, the mocking, and even the acceptance of the repercussions were a form of continued resistance by the prisoners. It was psychologically beneficial to the Poles to laugh at their captors' expense. This small effort brought a feeling of unity and spark of hope to the oppressed men.

The new cellmate continued with the most important bit of news. Jan was in a cell in the next hall, just on the other side of the wall.

Tears welled up in Józef's eyes with news of his brother, and a thought came to him. He asked a fellow prisoner to watch the hallway for any guards approaching. Józef took one of the metal soup cups and settled into the back corner of the room by the wall. He began to tap onto the block with concentration. Polish boy scouts all learned Morse code and practiced it in their games and field trips.

"Jan, this is your brother," he painstakingly completed. A few moments passed. No response. Józef repeated the tapped message and waited.

"Hello brother," came the tapped reply.

A rush of tears then flowed as their first contact in months finally broke a dam of fear and worry. Józef held his hands to his face for a few seconds, then he started tapping again.

"Did you talk?" he asked.

"I told them nothing," replied Jan.

"I knew it!" tapped Józef, exultant.

So it continued. Slowly and painstakingly the brothers communicated. Eventually, they hatched another better method of passing messages. Jan pilfered a couple sheets of paper from a trash bin in the interrogation room one morning while waiting for the questioners to arrive. Back at the cell he carefully folded and ripped them into small squares. With a tiny splinter of wood he used black grime from the floor to painstakingly write a tiny note. The prisoners were all taken once per day to a bathroom with a commode. While seated, Jan felt around the underside of the porcelain until he found a gap suitable for slipping the note and some sheets of blank paper. Later, he tapped the new secret to Józef using the Morse code. In this way they began passing written messages and dropped the dangerous and difficult tapping before getting caught.

They discussed the interrogation tactics and how best to counter them. They encouraged and buoyed each other's spirits. Staying stubborn and resolute was their plan, for as long as possible. Józef encouraged Jan to exercise, just in case an unlikely chance to escape developed.

Routinely, other prisoners were herded out in groups. The brothers could hear them being marched out into the center courtyard of the prison, followed by the shots that rang out as a firing squad liquidated the poor souls. One early morning Carp and Toad briskly walked up to the cell and opened the lock.

"Everyone out!" they shouted, and herded all six cellmates single file through the hall, down the stone steps, and into the courtyard where six guards with rifles stood waiting, looking bored and emotionless.

"Against the wall!" shouted Toad, as Carp began tying blindfolds over the face of each man. Józef was tied off and roughly jerked into place by the lumbering guards. He heard some emotional whimpers break from those around him. They stood on sticky congealed blood.

My God, he thought, *this is it. Their patience has run out.* He prayed and heard others whisper prayers. The unmistakable sound of bolt action mechanisms locking into place rang out.

Seconds passed. Then a minute, and another. A man was softly crying next to him, but otherwise it remained quiet. Another minute. Nothing. Ten minutes.

Józef was conscious of the morning sun hitting his face, having just crested the wall of the prison. He stood waiting. Suddenly, the blindfold was yanked off his face.

"Back to the cell!" came the order.

Once behind bars the prisoners all collapsed to the floor, a few wept openly. Józef sat quietly, completely drained. It had been just another psychological torture exercise.

The long damp winter painfully dragged on, its grayness and cold making prison existence even more difficult. Fellow prisoners increasingly became sick and died from illnesses and deprivation. Józef and a few others crafted a chess set out of bits of wood and concrete rubble. They marked out a game-board on the concrete floor. Playing chess then occupied endless hours and helped keep their mental faculties from declining.

They learned that in deep concentration one could push away the feelings of starvation and physical pain, at least for enough hours to get through another day. In addition to chess, the men joined in prayer often. They also discussed Polish literature and history.

Painstakingly, they recounted the stories from the Sienkiewicz 'Trilogy'. This was the great national trio of epic novels, describing the invasions of Poland in the mid-1600s, and the brave knights who fought for their homeland. One prisoner would start off and recount a portion of the story. Others would correct details as needed.

"Then, Pan Michael had a duel with Pan Andre," described one during his turn.

Another jumped in, "No, the duel came later, the knights were held in prison by Radziville first, and were sent away to be shot secretly, but Zagloba rescued them on the trip by convincing Kowalski that he was his uncle."

Everyone laughed remembering this part of the story.

"Oh yes, that's right, and then afterward Zagloba saves Pan Andre from the firing squad."

The current invasions struck everyone as the epic books coming to life, especially as in the middle volume, *The Deluge*, where Poland is weakened by eastern wars with Russians and Ukrainians, only to then be invaded by the Swedes from the west. Poland is almost defeated completely until holdout defenders of the Jasna Góra monastery, the home of the black Madonna icon, rally the country back to faith and patriotism. The way forward, as laid out in the two volumes of this middle book, was through complete self-sacrifice, bravery, and faithfulness.

And still the frequent interrogations in the middle of the night and occasional beatings continued. Józef and Jan saw fellow prisoners lose hope completely, then quickly decline and die. Some lost their minds first.

Throughout it all, Józef thought about the people holding him. The guards, like Carp and Toad, were really on the lowest rung of humanity he thought. Perhaps too stupid to feel any compassion or morality, they were just doing a job that fed their bellies, although he sensed that there was a factor of sadism that they enjoyed. They would have never had authority or power over anyone in a normal life due to their limited abilities, but here they enjoyed lording over the poor wretches placed under their fists and clubs.

The NKVD agents were another study. Were they true believers in the cause or just opportunistic career climbers? Either way, they were ruthless. The utilitarian view of humanity they seemed to hold was shocking.

What could make men into such creatures as this? Józef wondered.

At one point in the spring, Jan and Józef ended up on the same floor in the same hallway. From a few doors down Józef heard Jan engaging the guards Carp and Toad.

"How are your five year plans going? You're not as good at farming as the Polish nation is, I hear."

Carp answered angrily, "The crop yields are at record levels!" and waved a copy of his Soviet newspaper.

"I heard the cabbages all rotted last year," said Jan.

"That's a lie! The cabbage crop was at record levels!" Carp replied.

"But the wheat crop failed though, I can tell from this awful bread you give us," said Jan.

"Wheat was at record level!" the bovine-like guard shouted back. The prisoners up and down the hall were an appreciative audience to the conversation.

Józef leaned against the bars and joined in. "The problem with Russia is the fertilizer. You use any old crap, but good manure means good crops, that's why the best farmers use only *horse* manure in Poland. Personally, I prefer Arabian."

The guards just looked at him blankly, as the wheels in their brains turned ever so slowly.

"High class horses means high class manure means high class crops." Józef added.

"That's probably why your potato crop was down," said another prisoner, adding safety in numbers.

The guards were by then red faced and twitching.

"The potato crop was at record levels!"

"Not the oats, though," quietly added a fourth cellmate.

"The oat harvest was at record levels!" the angrily shouted reply came back.

"How about the beets? Not so good?" asked another, from the back of a cell.

"Beets were at record levels!" Carp yelled back.

"What about the oranges?" asked Jan.

"The orange crop was at record levels!" yelled the spitting mad Carp. This final ludicrous reply brought the entire cell block into waves of laughter that went on and on. Toad gripped his club and waved it at Jan but didn't attack as the embarrassment sank in.

The next day the men were served their bleak meal of bread and watery soup. Carp and Toad had almost left the hallway when an unknown prisoner called out, "What, no orange?"

The guards ran back as laughter again rang out from all the cells, showing their clubs and looking for the offender, but it was useless. Nearly every day at mealtime for several weeks, the guards would walk away after delivering the meager rations only to hear a voice call out, "You forgot my orange," followed by peals of laughter.

An old saying went around through the prisoners, "As long as we have a sense of humor, we are not defeated."

Spring warmth finally graced the land and the threat of disease and death seemed to ease a bit. The brothers were still hanging on to life, as for some reason the powers in control left it that way. It seemed a mystery. *Why were they so lucky?* There was no answer in this new world of random death. Eventually they would either die here or be sent to a gulag. That was the inevitable reality.

Chapter Five

German Attack - Death March

On June 22, 1941, what had seemed to be the inevitable fate changed. Air raid sirens screamed. The prisoners jumped up and began chattering. Shouts rang out in the hallways and back rooms of the prison complex. A sense of fear and chaos descended as guards and staff began running the halls. They seemed panicky and aimless, crossing back from where they just came, their eyes wide and terrified.

Explosions began sounding off in the distance, then closer. A tremendous crash rang out nearby, causing the smell of concrete dust and burnt wood to waft into the cells. The prisoners were yelling, pleading to be told what was happening. They overheard the shocking news from the hallways.

Germany was launching a full out blitzkrieg on Russia. The first waves of bombings were underway. Armored columns had crashed the border and were making headway fast, almost unopposed as the surprised Russian Army collapsed.

Shots rang out in the prison and Józef's heart sank. *They may shoot us all now,* he thought, *before they cut and run.* The other prisoners were screaming and shouting to be let out. Józef pressed against the bars and watched everything he could. The panic was palpable and no one seemed to be taking charge.

These damn jailers are a bunch of cowardly fools, he thought, *and they will all get killed.* Finally it was his old nemesis Vasily who showed up to give some orders. He was soaked with sweat and looked terrified. Arriving with a group of guards, he had them open the cells and run the prisoners out into the hallways, where they were funneled outside under more guards with submachine guns. A few prisoners drifted off from the group looking for an escape, and were immediately gunned down, dropping in bloody heaps. The guards shouted at the rest, their eyes looking wild and deadly. It was total chaos.

Józef stayed tight to the group, which was increasing in size to hundreds of prisoners. He looked for Jan. His senses were heightened and he began keenly observing all around him. Vasily and several other NKVD officers were off to the side in a group, arms gesticulating and pointing in different directions. It did not look under control. Guards surrounded the prisoners looking scared and trigger happy.

Józef felt a hand grasp his shoulder from behind. It was Jan.

"Thank God!" he exclaimed. They locked eyes with hands on each other's shoulders for a brief moment.

The orders sounded out from the guards, having finally received some direction by the hapless officers. The prisoners were being marched off, evacuating the prison, and heading east away from the front. As they moved off, some semblance of organization set in. A line of four to five men wide was arranged as it snaked off into the distance. Guards walked along the outside edges along the whole length.

Jan and Józef found themselves in the middle of the group of hundreds of prisoners moving forward. A man near them suddenly bolted, running for freedom, but was immediately riddled with bullets and fell. A guard with a rifle walked over and administered a final shot to the head.

"Stay with me," Józef said to Jan. "Our chance will come."

The pace was brisk. It was almost like a run. Fear was driving everyone as the sound of shelling continued, but it was too fast paced of a march, and inevitably, weaker men began fading. They started limping and then drifting back through the line. Initially, there was shouting by the guards to keep up, but after a while rifle shots rang out with frequency. The weak and slow, once falling far enough behind, were being dispatched.

It was an agonizing first few hours, as the pattern continued. A man, face twisted with exertion, looked helplessly at the other prisoners passing him by as he disappeared into the rear of the column. The crack of a rifle, and sometimes a groan, ended each drama at random intervals.

As another weakening man passed through, Jan suddenly grabbed his arm and helped him along. Józef quickly took up the other arm. They lifted up his weight a bit but he soon began struggling more, breathing in gasps and limping terribly. A guard stepped closer to the three, unsure for the moment what to do. Then he yelled out in Russian, "No help!"

Jan and Józef retained the grip, unwilling to let go. The struggling man looked at them both and shook his head. He pulled away his arms and flowed back through the column like a struggling fish in a stream. A few moments later a single shot ended another life.

Half a day of agony continued on the hot dusty road. The pace slowed and the shooting ended as only stronger men were left. Thirst and bodily aches set upon all the prisoners. The walk continued all day and into the evening. Arriving at a small village, they were herded into a wire fenced pen between two one-story buildings. They were ordered to sit down and guards were set up on the perimeters. The Poles watched as their Russian captors had food and water, but the prisoners received nothing. Józef and Jan sat close and talked about possibilities for escape, then settled down on the dusty ground and slept a few hours.

At dawn the sound of bomb blasts commenced. Although the explosions seemed far away, the panicked Russians got them up and marching quickly. A few prisoners, having pushed themselves to the limit the day before, could not get up and stand, much less march. Short bursts of gunfire punctuated the distant bomb blasts as they were summarily executed.

Another hot day of walking strained the prisoners. The dry dusty road aggravated their incredible thirst, and they begged the guards to let them drink from a nearby stream. The guards finally relented and allowed the men to briefly run to the stream's edge where they lay on their stomachs side by side and scooped handfuls of water. It was life saving.

But not everyone returned to the march. Sustained machine gun fire was heard to the rear. The Russians had decided to randomly cull the herd. An unknown number of prisoners were shuffled off to the side after the water break and massacred.

As the day wore on the sound of bombing continued to be heard, but not always from behind, and the guards became increasingly agitated. Józef overheard them grumbling about this task. They were suggesting a better plan would be to finish off all the prisoners and travel more quickly on their own. He and Jan vowed to find an escape soon.

The brutal death march continued well into darkness before they arrived at another prison. This one had ten foot high fencing with barbed wire at the top and a guard tower at the gate. At the end was a barracks-type building where the Russians entered after posting guards. The prisoners were left outside in the fenced area. They again received no food or water.

Józef and Jan milled around the yard but they were actually scouting the surroundings. To the north, east and west were rather open streets with small impoverished looking houses, but to the south was an inviting tract of woods. The brothers, locked away in cement block rooms for so many months, stared longingly at the beautiful leafy woods. They quietly discussed escape scenarios for some time, then gave into exhaustion and stretched out on the hard-packed dirt to sleep a little.

The morning broke and Józef was up instantly with eyes wide open. He had a palpable sense of energy. His brother looked at him, also wide eyed and seemingly ready for action. It was a wartime situation that he would experience repeatedly over the coming years, but Józef didn't yet know what to make of it. They stood up and scanned the brightening yard.

A faint buzzing sound came to their ears and they strained to look around at the sky. *There...* two distant specks came into focus at the misty horizon. *Planes.* They watched the aircraft approach, transfixed. The rest of the yard and barracks seemed quiet and peaceful. A light was on in the barracks and they caught a glimpse of some movement inside.

Bastards are probably getting some nice breakfast, Józef thought. He turned back, and the two planes were flying nearer quickly, then the engines gunned and they rocketed high into the sky. The sudden explosive roar woke up the whole camp. Guards ran out of the barracks to look. Prisoners were standing up everywhere.

Józef recognized the planes as German Stuka dive bombers. The planes finished their steep loud climb and arched into their characteristic dive. The boys sensed running and panic all around the yard, but were so spellbound that they momentarily just stood still and watched. The bombers raced towards earth at an impossibly steep angle.

The terrible Stuka screaming sound snapped the brothers out of inaction and they ran from their spot and away from the planes' path. Looking up they saw the wobbling bombs leave the planes and straighten out for a second before several concussive explosions impacted.

The explosions knocked Józef and Jan off their feet, but they were able to get up instantly, as adrenaline pumped them full of unexpected strength. The south corner of the barracks was blown up and in flames. A direct hit. Black billowing smoke obscured half the building. The other blast seemed to fall just behind the camp, where another fire then raged.

Józef scanned the yard intently as the Stukas began circling around for another pass. Guards ran about frantically, uselessly firing at the oncoming planes with rifles. The raging flames, the screaming of injured men, and the again diving Stukas created a hellish cacophony of sound, and then Józef saw what he was looking for. The flames and smoke parted for a brief second, enough to see that the fence in the area where it had attached to the barracks was gone.

Józef grabbed Jan's arm and they ran towards the newly formed gap. They sprinted the short distance towards the breach, which was fully engulfed in smoke again. The corner of the building was an inferno, but they hit the opening fast and leaped over the charred timbers. For a moment they disappeared into black oily smoke, then emerged from darkness into light.

They ran for the woods. Legs pumping they continued the effort, and reached the tree line, a herculean task after the exertion of the death march.

"Farther!" Józef urged as they kept going into the forest. After a few moments they couldn't run any longer, but kept up a fast walk. They could not speak, as even a word would take too much energy, but kept up a stumbling forward progress. They both began falling down, struggling to get up and keep moving, but their legs kept giving out. Deeper into this woodland they pushed. Finally, having reached the limit of endurance, they scrambled down a ravine, and hid beneath some low hanging evergreens. They looked at each other, scarcely believing what had just happened. Off in the distance, they heard the Stukas dive bombing the town.

Józef lay flat and peered out from their hiding spot until he saw that no one was following them. Completely exhausted, they rested in place, as they simply could not go on.

Despite his physical collapse, Józef's mind raced. He thought about what the guards at the prison were experiencing. Józef was convinced the fearful and chaotic Russians would not waste time and energy chasing down a couple scraggly escaped prisoners, if they had even been noticed at all. The Russians were too busy running for their lives from the German onslaught. The brothers had truly escaped.

Chapter Six

ANOTHER JOURNEY HOME

THE JOURNEY HOME started that afternoon. They had fallen asleep for some period of time. Józef woke up first, and realized that Jan was sleeping against his shoulder, just like so many times when they were little boys, napping on their sofa after playing hard all day. He nudged Jan awake.

Their training and experience kicked in immediately as they discussed the needs of food, shelter, and navigation. Extreme caution had to be exercised since any human contact could lead to grave danger when in enemy and war torn territory. Locals could report them to authorities or they could get spotted by German troops. Józef felt confident in their ability to stay hidden while traveling, but the need for real nutrition was pressing, given their weakened state. That could only come from human sources.

In desperation, they decided to approach a tiny farmstead that evening. First they scouted it out from a distance. There was an old farmer and his wife, but no others. The house and small barn were isolated and alone. They stepped out when the old farmer started walking towards the barn.

"Hello" Józef called out.

The escapees walked up calmly, exposing the palms of their hands, trying to look as unthreatening as possible. The farmer was startled. He walked quickly to the barn and picked up a pitchfork, which he didn't lift up, but just held to his side. Józef and Jan put a gentle smile on, but their haggard and emaciated appearance must have been alarming.

"We are just passing by," Józef said in broken Russian. "Can you spare just a bit of food?"

The farmer didn't speak, but motioned for them to stop and wait. Then he ducked into the barn. He walked back out in a minute, still holding the pitchfork, but with the other hand he held out two fresh eggs and one head of old looking raw cabbage. He handed the food to Jan and backed away, then emphatically motioned for them to leave.

Józef thanked him, gave him a respectful bow, and then walked away quickly. They moved on, stopping briefly to crack and suck down an egg each, and then split the cabbage. It was a glorious, wonderful meal.

The journey continued with several similar exchanges. Sometimes they snuck into farm plots at night and rooted out a few vegetables, gaining just enough calories to keep them going. Habitations that looked risky were avoided. Too many people around meant too many eyes that could spot them, too many mouths to potentially report them.

The brothers were able to beg for some food at different, less populated stops. They supplemented their diet with any opportunity. Using their experience they gathered a few crayfish from a little brook and ate the tails raw. There were berries and other woodland edibles to be found along the route. Even though they were walking all day, every day, they gained strength. The miracle of freedom shared together on this road lifted them up, and gave them the energy to continue.

They grew even closer than before on the long walk, discussing the recent ordeal, but also talking about life in general, and recounting memories from the past as they shared in the blessing of brotherhood.

"Józef, tell me about you and the wolf again," asked Jan. "I haven't heard that story in years."

"Ok," Józef answered as they made their way through an open, lovely area of giant trees. "I was nine years old, and was hiking through that big woodland between our house and the Naliboki forest. I had checked my snare traps but had no luck, when it started to rain. It was a soft rain, but was increasing, so I thought I would wait it out under shelter. There was a giant oak tree there, with a big hollowed out section on one side, so I got inside and sat down, almost completely hidden from the outside. As I sat and waited, I was startled to see a wolf walk into the little glade, and sit down just thirty feet away. It just sat there, calmly looking here and there, apparently taking a rest where the big tree canopies kept it a little dry."

Jan glanced at his brother as Józef continued.

"I started shaking with fear and prayed it would not spot me before it wandered away. Suddenly and horrifyingly, I felt the terrible urge to sneeze. I held it back with all my might, pinching my face with total effort. The feeling left, and I thought I had dodged a bullet, when it suddenly came back, more intense than before, and I couldn't stop from releasing a loud *'AH CHOO!'*

"The wolf jumped up and landed on all fours with death and fear in its eyes, and looked right at me, baring its teeth. I clambered out, screaming in terror, and started running hard for home. As I ran, I could feel not only branches whipping my body but also was sure that I felt the wolf snapping at the back of my legs. I could not look back. As I left the woods edge and was in sight of our house I started screaming, *'Wolf! Wolf! Open the door! Open the door!'* I saw Dad in the distance open the door and just look at me, perplexed. I ran wildly with my last bit of strength and literally dove into the house and rolled across the floor."

Jan's face reflected not the peril of his brother, but the humor of the upcoming story's finale, one he had heard many times.

"For a few seconds," Józef went on, "everyone just stared at me before they started laughing hysterically. Dad just calmly said 'there is no wolf out there.' Everyone had a good time chuckling and describing my terrified run and wild yelling about a non-existent wolf. I realized then that the poor animal had probably been as scared as me, and had likely run the opposite direction–"

"Yes, that's very likely," Jan interrupted, "nobody else can sneeze as loud as you! I would have been scared too!"

Józef chuckled, nodding. "I was the butt of jokes for this escapade for many years. I would get so mad and embarrassed, until I grew up a little, saw the humor in it, and started telling the story myself."

Jan laughed and they walked on a bit.

"Your turn, Jan. Tell me again about dunking the girls," Józef demanded.

Jan smiled coyly, and then slipped into his own adventurous tale. "Well, the two girls arrived at the pre-wedding activities looking very finely dressed and all made up. They were really a sight to see, but they obviously knew it. Their dresses were fancy and looked expensive. Perhaps they got them from a bigger city on some trip. A lot of us from school gathered together and were having fun, but it seemed that many of the other girls were annoyed. These two were subtly mocking the other girls modest outfits as they pranced around proudly. Of course, girls always notice these things. Feelings were hurt."

"Of course," Józef interjected.

"Eventually, after the ceremony," Jan continued, "there was a pretty long wait milling around before dinner. I suggested that I could take the two girls out on a little rowboat ride. They were agreeable. Naturally, I had picked them, they must have thought, since they were outshining all the others. I rowed out a little way and we sat in the beautiful sunshine, as the girls that had been left behind cast glances our way."

"As can only be expected from the other girls," Józef added.

Jan looked at his brother, and continued, "My passengers had probably hit the peak of their prideful contentment when I suddenly announced 'It's hot, time for a dip!' and stood on the gunwale, which tipped the boat over, and we all went right in. We were only in three feet of water, so they quickly stood up, but were now looking like angry wet cats that had been thrown in a pond. All I could hear was their screaming at me above the laughter and pointing coming from shore. To tell you the truth, I immediately felt terrible. It was really an impulsive thing I did, but I had to run away from their slaps and blows. Much later, when they arrived at the wedding after re-dressing completely, I approached them and apologized. At first they just gave me icy stares, but by the end of the night, I actually danced a couple songs with each of them, and forgiveness for an old friend was allowed."

"People still talk about it a lot around town," Józef replied, grinning and shaking his head.

"Remember when we won the orienteering contest with the scouts?" asked Jan.

"Yes," Józef replied, "We cheated."

"We absolutely did not cheat, we were just better woodsmen," said Jan.

"Ok, I guess I can go along with that account," laughed Józef.

The big end of the season contest for that scouting year was the mapping and orienteering challenge. The brothers were one of five two-man teams in the final test. The trophy cup was much desired by everyone.

On the day of the event the teams met at the edge of the Naliboki forest and the scoutmaster unveiled the maps with the target marked in a red "X". Each team had only a map and a compass. When shown the map Józef and Jan could barely contain themselves, and wouldn't even make eye contact with each other for fear of bursting out laughing. The goal was an old set of ruins. It was an old partial wall and fireplace of fieldstone in a small dry area where two small streams converged. The boys had literally been there a hundred times. No one spent as much time wandering the woods as these two boys had.

They had another advantage also. In their frequent hikes, the boys had discovered a straight path through the swamp. The challenge of this contest was circling either right or left around a huge wetland while keeping one's bearings to get to the ruins. The Niedźwieckis learned after many previous attempts that they could avoid two hours of travel by jumping from dry spot to spot for a ways, then traversing a narrow trail, and then performing one final trick. No one knew that in midsummer when the woods were at its driest period a ridge of damp but walkable ground appeared and cut a path through what everyone else thought was deep water. On their many hunting and trapping trips this discovery saved them almost four hours of walking to get to prime hunting and trapping grounds.

The contest started with everyone running. Every team was confident and didn't want any followers stealing their sure win. Jan and Józef let everyone else get a head start. Then they quickly took their secret path and arrived at the ruins in an hour. They never even pulled out the map or compass. Then they waited. And waited.

After two hours the scoutmaster and his assistant arrived with the first excited team right behind. Józef leaned against the ruins, acting bored and pretending to be reading a small copy of *"With Fire and Sword."* Jan was laying on the ground with a straw hat pulled down over his face making exaggerated snoring sounds, as if sound asleep. The scoutmaster looked completely stunned, but the other arriving team of scouts went from exultation to blubbering tears instantly. As each crew appeared, a boy from that first team ran out to announce tearfully to them, "The Niedźwieckis have been here for hours!"

The trophy cup came home to sit on the Niedźwiecki fireplace mantle, the great prize of that fourth year of scouting.

The brothers continued their travels. Despite the relief and joy of being free, the nightmares and flashbacks of prison and the march would haunt the boys many times a day for several months. They woke up in the mornings expecting a dead corpse next to them, sitting up suddenly until realizing they were in the woods, well away from any Russians.

When they arrived in Polish territory they hitched rides on a truck and then a wagon to help the journey along. It took weeks to arrive back home. On a warm midsummer day in Iwieniec, a young voice pierced the hazy July calm. A seven-year-old nephew breathlessly ran to the Niedźwiecki house, his bare feet sending little clouds of dust swirling across the dirt road.

"The boys are coming home!" he shouted out repeatedly as he raced to their door. Everyone reacted with stunned disbelief and confusion. Helena dropped a plate she was washing and it smashed on the floor.

"They are walking down the road, Józef and Janusch are coming home," the boy yelled, his face shining with excitement as he pointed up the street. The brothers had not been expected to be seen ever again, as no one ever came back from NKVD prison, definitely not after so many months. The stunned household jumped up, first one, then another and another, as they came out of their shocked paralysis and rushed out the door, where Jan and Józef could be seen striding towards them, gaunt and bony looking, as if returning from the dead.

Everyone hugged and sobbed in an emotional reunion in the street, joined by some equally shocked and happy neighbors. Months of oppressive sadness had been suddenly lifted for the tight knit family as the boys, thought lost forever, were home.

Around the region, the German attack had pushed the Russians out of the occupied areas of Poland. The numerous NKVD prisons were abandoned and left behind. In most cases the prisoners were all killed beforehand. Local townspeople arrived to find horrible scenes of shot or poisoned friends and family members. Hideous examples of inflicted torture were observed.

Very few prisoners were marched away and kept alive as in the case of the Niedźwiecki brothers. Very, very few then escaped the death marches without dying along the way or being massacred.

Józef and Jan had been told by Vasily that it was a man named Biały that had given them up by tipping off the NKVD. They planned to find him and administer street justice at the first chance. They had suffered too much to not have their revenge. They talked openly about it.

Just a few days after their return, a knock came to the door. Helena opened it and Józef and Jan were surprised to see none other than Biały standing there. He stepped inside quickly and immediately dropped to his knees and put his hands up. In a sobbing voice he launched into a desperate apologetic outburst.

"I was beaten!" Biały exclaimed, "And they were threatening my family!" Józef and Jan, completely stunned, were speechless.

"Please don't kill me!" he sobbed, as he continued describing the desperate spot he had been put in.

The brothers, having not betrayed a single person during their lengthy ordeal, were not initially moved to pity, but were not inclined to violence toward a begging, crying man. Biały grabbed at Józef's hand, tears flowing from his eyes. Józef pulled it away.

"We are not going to kill you," Józef eventually answered. He then told Biały that he would possibly face justice from the underground, but for now to leave and go home. Although hardened by the ordeal of their imprisonment, Józef and Jan never followed up on their vow to kill Biały.

The boys had suffered greatly. They had cheated death through good fortune, God's grace, and their own strength. They had to decide what to do with this gift of life. They could lay low and hide out. They could certainly run away and disappear from the area for good. They decided instead to rejoin the underground and continue the fight for their homeland.

Chapter Seven

Conspiracy

IWIENIEC WAS THEN under German occupation. Józef and Jan learned about the new situation as they recovered their health and strength. They heard how the Jewish population was being rounded up, and most likely all sent to ghettos or concentration camps. The budding Polish underground tried to help, but no one expected the speed and finality of what happened to their Jewish neighbors.

Further complicating the picture in the region were the Soviet partisans. The Nazi invasion had moved so fast that thousands of Russians were stranded behind in what was by then German occupied territory. They retreated to the woods and small towns and hid out in groups that turned into red partisan units. A big home base for them was the nearby Naliboki forest, a large wilderness area full of bogs and swamps, old growth timber, and few roads.

The Russian partisan units were not engaging in actions against the Germans in the early days of occupation, instead they were concerned mostly with just surviving. But they were harassing the local Polish populace with constant robbery of food and supplies. The need for a Polish response to protect the oppressed locals became an urgent concern, and hastened the formation of the new underground Home Army group

Meanwhile in town, the Germans were instituting a rigid and brutal regime of their own. At its head was Chief Karl Sawinola. His actual name was "Karl Cavill" but he was called "Sawinola," or "Czech" because his name sounded like a Czechoslovakian name to the Poles.

Czech was a sadistic and cruel man. To compound his murderous instincts, Czech was a heavy drinker who showed signs of intoxication early most days. Scaffolds went up in the center of town where arrested men and women were hung frequently. Firing squads supplied even more victims.

Czech became known for repeating what he thought was a clever and funny saying. When greeted on the street or in his office with "How do you do?" or "How are you today?" His response was a version of "I feel awful, I haven't killed anyone yet today," followed by a chuckle.

The head of the new local Polish underground unit was Kacper Miłaszewski, a former reserve lieutenant in the Polish Army. He spoke perfect Russian and began negotiating with the Russian partisans right away. Areas of influence were designated and protections demanded for local civilians.

When Aleksander Warakomski, a district commander was sent to the region in 1942 to help form an underground, he found an already operating unit set up by Miłaszewski.

From a group of about forty core people, by the spring of 1943 they had increased to well over two hundred men and women, and serious military action was now on the table. Early plans were discussed to attack the Nazi garrison in Iwieniec. With a successful attack, the underground hoped to gain enough weapons and supplies to take the jump from ragtag partisans to a real fighting force.

Another goal was to put an end to the murderous reign of Czech. It was a policy of the underground all over Poland to eliminate the most brutal Nazi officials. It forced the next leader in charge to think twice about the murder of innocent civilians.

Miłaszewski, even though his underground unit was just getting started, made every effort to help the local Jewish citizens. He sent word to them when intelligence contacts warned of German actions, and even arranged to sneak some Jews out of the ghetto when an opportunity presented itself

To protect their identities and family members, the underground members chose *noms-de-guerre*. Miłaszewski was

"*Lewald.*" Józef chose "*Szary,*" which translates to "*Gray.*" Jan Niedźwiecki, true to form, chose the dramatic "*Piorun*" or "*Thunderbolt.*"

Thunderbolt needed a new horse and the underground set him up to get one from the Kul estate. The Niedźwiecki brothers went out together and arrived to check out the horse barn. They entered and headed down separate sides of the barn looking at each stall. As Jan walked along looking to the left, a horse suddenly jutted its head out from the right and bumped Jan hard in the chest.

"Woah," Jan exclaimed, "what's that about?" The two new acquaintances eyed each other, before Jan said, "You really look like something."

"Did you already pick one?" Józef shouted out.

"I think one picked me," Jan replied.

As Józef exited the barn Jan was already leading a big and muscular black horse outside. He saddled it up, put his leg in a stirrup and jumped on, then began trotting around turning left and right.

"Take it easy at first," Józef suggested, just as Jan kicked the horse into a hard gallop and began racing around the corral. The horse was impressive in speed and power. Józef watched as Jan sped towards the fence, then leaped it easily, landing gracefully and then galloping off across the meadow. Józef just shook his head at his reckless brother, but could see it was truly a special animal.

When Jan returned he announced that this was his new horse. They rode home together and Jan was beaming with joy.

"What will you name him?" asked Józef.

"Bucephalus," Jan answered directly.

"Of course!" responded Józef, laughing and slapping his leg, recalling the great stories told to them by one of their childhood history teachers. Bucephalus was the battle horse of Alexander the Great.

As the weeks went on Józef observed that the big strong horse was actually a little hard to control. It was willful and sometimes obstinate, but it could run like the wind.

He may not be the best partisan horse, Józef thought, as quick and efficient responses were so often needed in battle.

One day as the brothers rode along together, Józef observed how Bucephalus continued to resist the first directions from Jan. Sometimes, if the horse wanted to go a different direction than pulled, he would shake his head and loudly protest. Józef was worried and wanted to talk to Jan about it, so thought for a few minutes about how to best start. Then he began.

"Jan, if you were about to charge down the Kahlenberg, and smash into the camp of Kara Mustafa Pasha," Józef referred to the famous Polish Winged Hussar charge that lifted the siege of Vienna in 1683, "this horse could no doubt have led the assault, and King Sobieski himself would have watched him from far behind."

"I knew this was coming," said Jan, "go ahead with the *but*."

"But..." Józef said, "we need quick and quiet obedience from our horses in partisan warfare."

"I realize everything you are saying. I am trying to break him of his bad habits. I will give him a little more time. Maybe he can be great. I promise I won't take too long."

The underground organization started planting people in various roles that could help in future actions. Józef's sister Rufina Niedźwiecka was a key person, as she got a job as a clerk right in Chief Sawinola's office. With incredible bravery she secretly passed warnings out to the underground, saving many from arrest or torture.

Józef had status in the local area, as the famous soldier who escaped not once, but twice from Soviet captivity, in addition to taking part in the defense of Poland in 1939. He was tapped for leadership right away. Word of the new resistance group spread quickly and volunteers made contact from many nearby towns.

The tenuous working relationship with the Soviets soured when Russian partisans attacked and massacred the Polish defense unit and townspeople in the town of Naliboki. The residents had created an armed self defense force and denied Russian partisans access to their food and shelter. The angered Russians responded with arson and murder. The urgency to have a real Polish counterforce grew.

The brothers stopped staying at home and began living in safe houses in the country. Training with the underground occupied their time. They occasionally ventured into Iwieniec on reconnaissance missions to observe the Germans and meet with other underground members.

On one such foray they hid at the outskirts of the Orthodox cemetery and observed Czech and a dozen gendarmes march some prisoners in. The cemetery was an execution zone for the Nazi regime. Jan gasped as he noticed one of his school friends in the group of prisoners.

Józef recognized him also.

"What the hell did they grab him for?" Jan hissed through his teeth. "He wouldn't hurt a fly, and he isn't in the underground."

The young man had been arrested by the German authorities for helping a Jew, but the boys didn't know this at the time. He had tried to smuggle a friend out of town and to the forest in a hay wagon, but had been spotted by an informant.

The prisoners were quickly lined up, but Czech held up the process. His movements suggested that he was intoxicated, as usual. Czech directed the prisoners to be lined up in a single file, instead of lined up in a row. Then he ordered a single rifleman to fire at the first man in line. A shot rang out and the first two men in line dropped. The second man was still writhing in pain on the ground.

Czech was playing a game for his own amusement. He wanted to see how many men a single bullet could kill after passing through the first body. Czech finished off the injured man with his pistol. The guards lined up another try, this time with Jan's friend in front. Jan made a muffled sound of anguish and Józef swore under his breath. Jan could see the fearful contorted face of his friend, and had to resist the urge to charge out and intervene. Józef gripped his arm tightly, partially in shared grief but also in fear of Jan making a foolhardy move.

The executioner fired. Jan's friend and the next two men behind him fell. Czech motioned to his men and they quickly lined up the prisoners in a normal line. Several rifles raised and dispatched all the remaining men. It was a grotesque and haphazard execution, very different from the typical efficient German methods. But this was part of life under the hard drinking sadist, Chief Sawinola.

Many more of the boys' friends would end up victims of the Nazi occupation in town. Every witnessed shooting and hanging steeled the resolve of the brothers for the upcoming action, especially the terrible sight of young women at the end of the rope, swaying in their soft dresses, their deaths wickedly displayed as a warning to the terrorized populace.

Tentative plans to attack the Iwieniec garrison were formed for early June, then canceled when the Germans were alerted. Then a plan was formed for June 22. But disaster struck during this period of planning. The German authorities, aware of the new Polish unit, had been stalking the new conspiracy through Gestapo spies, which culminated in a mass arrest of eighty members in a successful sweep. The arrested were held in Iwieniec at the Belarussian Police force station prison. Polish inside sources warned that the situation was dire. The prisoners would be herded off to the woods for liquidation within days.

The German command at this time had also called for a roundup of all young men of the area. They were to gather in town on June 19 and report to the headquarters for either conscription or for forced labor in Germany. The penalty for not complying was always the same under Nazi occupation - death.

A call for horses to be brought in to be "bought" for the German army also was ordered for the same day. These orders created an opportunity for the underground. The Polish leadership started developing a plan to use the inflow of men and horses as cover for a military action on the 19th. The new objectives were to rescue the prisoners and stop the conscription of the men, in addition to destroying the German garrison, getting weapons and equipment, and lastly, eliminating the killer Czech, Chief Sawinola.

The underground had been analyzing every routine of the German movements in Iwieniec: when and where guards were posted, their shift changes, the times of meals and meetings, and every bit of information on where weapons could be quickly acquired. Training took place out in the country at secret locations.

The enemy forces in Iwieniec included one hundred German gendarmes, three hundred Belarussian police, and one hundred other miscellaneous German economic staff. To complicate matters, there were two hundred and fifty Luftwaffe soldiers stationed at a barracks two kilometers away on leave for rest. This was a very significant force to overcome for the lightly armed partisans, so the initial action plan needed to be a complete surprise. The Poles numbered approximately one hundred and fifty men, lightly armed against six hundred fortified Nazi troops. Only a meticulous and audacious sudden attack would work.

Miłaszewski led the planning group, which included the following members: Olgierd Woyno - "*Lech,*" Walenty Parchimowicz - "*Walden,*" Zdzisław Nurkiewicz - "*Noc,*" Jan Jakubowski - "*Dab,*" and the Niedźwiecki brothers - "*Szary,*" and "*Piorun.*"

First, all communication lines to the outside world needed to be eliminated. Any quick reinforcement or aid to the enemy would end the Poles' hopes quickly. The gendarmerie, the Belarus police station, the German economic offices, and the Luftwaffe barracks had to be hit swiftly and simultaneously. All guards and sentries had to be taken out early. The Belarus police were heavily infiltrated by Polish underground members and many others' loyalty to Germany was suspect, so that was counted on to help alleviate the odds. The Belarus Police allies pilfered a few German weapons to aid the underground in the attack.

The plans were run through repeatedly. Over and over members were quizzed as to their task, and all the details clarified. The most dangerous task of all was the initial attack on the gendarmerie building. Someone would have to charge the front entrance, catch the Germans by surprise in the main room where lunch was served, and divert attention from an attack on the radio station on the second floor of the gendarmerie. It was crucial that the communication center in the building be destroyed in the first moments.

The gendarmerie was surrounded by earthworks except for the narrow front walk. It was decided a small group would enter the gendarmerie first, one man at the main entrance and two would sneak in the side to destroy the radio station. A full assault would have been spotted quickly and stopped. A team of attackers would follow seconds behind the first man, hoping to eliminate a large number of gendarmes and win the building quickly. It was observed that the noon meal was the absolute weakest moment of German vigilance during an average day.

There were several volunteers to be this first man in. The Niedźwiecki brothers were among them. It was decided that the volunteers would pull matchsticks to determine who would get this hazardous mission. Miłaszewski turned his back to the others in order to set up the contest, and then faced them again holding out the open matchbox. Józef pulled first and retrieved a long match stick. Two others also drew long and were not selected. Jan Niedźwiecki then drew the short straw with his turn. He would be the one to charge the entrance of the gendarmerie.

This upset Józef immensely, and he begged Jan to trade places. He had a bad feeling, almost a premonition of doom. Jan refused. He wanted this important job and was proud to do it. Józef's multiple requests were rebuffed. "This is my task," Jan said, "I will hit them like a *thunderbolt*," he followed up, with a glint in his eye and a quick laugh.

"I have more fighting experience," Józef implored, "please, please, let's switch missions."

"Not a chance, brother," replied Jan. "I can do it, and besides, I have been to Father Hilary for confession and am in a good place, and you have not, you heathen."

"Will you change spots if I go confess right now?" asked Józef.

"No, brother, but you should go anyway."

On June 18th, the night before the planned attack, Józef, Jan and several others gathered in the Niedźwiecki home, and officially took the oath to the Home Army. All the men and witnesses bore upon their faces the seriousness and gravity of the situation. With hands on crucifix and rosary, they read the words in turn, pledging to fight for their country, before God, loyal to death.

Oath to the Home Army

"Before God Almighty
and Mary the Blessed Virgin,
Queen of the Polish Crown.
I pledge allegiance to my Motherland,
The Republic of Poland.

I pledge to steadfastly guard her honor,
and to fight for her liberation
with all my strength,
even to the extent of
sacrificing my own life.

I pledge unconditional obedience to
the President of Poland,
the Commander in Chief of
the Republic of Poland,
and to the Home Army Commander.
I promise to keep secret whatever
may happen to me. So help me God."

Chapter Eight

THE IWIENIEC UPRISING

THE MORNING OF JUNE 19, 1943 saw the partisans up early and preparing for battle. Half the forces would stream into town in plain clothes, taking advantage of the German order. The other half had to stealthily move into their attack positions on the outskirts of town and around the Luftwaffe barracks. Cavalry troops would move into place to guard roads against any possible German reinforcements. Everyone mentally walked through their specific tasks. Weapons and ammo were in very short supply so would have to be used efficiently until German arms were seized.

It was a beautiful warm summer day of blue skies and no clouds. Men and horses were filtering in as local Poles and Belarusians followed the German orders.

Józef led a group from his camp near Lake Kroman to Iwieniec in the mid-morning. They hid in the wooded Jewish cemetery and waited. His carefully cleaned and loaded pistol was in a holster on his belt.

Jan strode into town unarmed with just a light vest over his shirt. As he approached the last few blocks he checked his watch. The attack would start when the church bells rang out at the noon Angelus. Once the entrance was breached and the radio station taken out, a full out assault would commence from the groups led by *"Lech"* and Sgt. Walerian Żuchowicz – *"Opończa."*

Jan was a bit early so he slowed his pace. He stopped at a store window and pretended to peruse the sparse merchandise on display. He checked his watch again, then realized that this was a nervous, suspicious-looking behavior. He started walking his route again.

Jan made the last turn between some houses and paused. At his side two men appeared. Jan Misiaczek and Jan Bryczkowski were also dressed in civilian clothes. In training sessions they had joked about the "three Jans" who made up this forward team. Misiaczek was a telephone worker in civilian life and knew the location and layout of the radio station in the gendarmerie.

Halfway down the street a curtain moved slightly as someone watched their approach. The men paused as two wooden window shutters opened at street level, and a carbine was quietly lowered out and leaned against the wall below. Then a shorter, fully automatic German MP-40 submachine gun appeared and was placed alongside. Finally, a basket with a cloth, as if prepared for Easter, was lowered down.

The Jans moved forward now. One of the men lifted the white embroidered cloth of the basket to reveal four grenades nestled within like eggs. Two each for Misiaczek and Bryczkowski. Jan Niedźwiecki picked up the carbine and slung the machine gun over his shoulder as they walked away. Jan had chosen the carbine for accuracy outside, and the machine gun for volume of fire once inside. The basket was then hoisted back through the window and the shutters quickly closed and locked by the unseen patriot. A few hundred feet away they spotted *Opończa*, who gave them the sign that everyone was in place.

Suddenly, the first bell of the Angelus at St Michael's rang out. It was the signal. It seemed early, throwing off their timing, but the three men instantly started running towards the target. As soon as they hit the open space in front of the large building, Jan Niedźwiecki looked up to see the German lookout in the cupola on the roof. The lookout was already staring at the three armed men as Niedźwiecki lifted his carbine. He aimed, let out his breath, held, and fired twice. The lookout's body jerked as the bullets struck and he slumped out of view.

Thunderbolt then set down the carbine and took up the machine gun, charging up the front walk. In his peripheral vision he was aware of his partners full out sprinting to the left and around the corner of the building. He bounded up the steps, opened the front door and burst into the gendarmerie, the machine gun aimed from the hip. In the large and open entrance room there were a half dozen German soldiers milling around waiting for their midday meal. There were fewer men than expected, because of the early bell. They all turned to look after the door violently swung open.

Jan opened fire instantly, and the victims tumbled over tables and chairs. He hesitated for a moment, surveying the blood splattered room and the sprawled bodies for signs of life. Nothing. Seconds later a terrific explosion rocked the building, causing dust to fall from the ceiling.

Misiaczek and Bryczkowski had broken a side window and entered, then sprinted up the stairs to the second floor. They ran to the radio station room as they pulled the pins on their grenades. Upon entering the room there was a brief and odd moment as the radio operator, already attempting to contact the German garrison in Stołpce, turned in his chair and looked at the two guests with fear and surprise. Misiaczek, followed by Bryczkowski, dropped their grenades on the floor and dashed across the room to the open window. Misiaczek shimmied down the gutter pipe to the ground below. Bryczkowski was half way down when the thunderous explosion sent pieces of furniture and radio station out the window and over their heads.

All around Iwieniec pistols were drawn and placed at the heads of German guards at the first bell sound. The guards were quickly disarmed and brought away from the battle to a holding area. Each team of partisans sprang into action.

Jan Jakubowski's group ran to the Belarus police station and tried to disarm the two sentries, who resisted and were killed. The men then surrounded the building and called for surrender. The head of the police was not present so the second in command, who was a member of the underground, ordered surrender and had the men file out. A few true loyalists to the Germans started fighting though, and they were killed in a short battle. The Poles quickly grabbed up weapons from the armory to send out across the growing battle. The prison cells were unlocked and the underground members ran out to join the fight.

Two kilometers away Miłaszewski and Parchimowicz led the attack on the Luftwaffe barracks. They surrounded the buildings and began firing at the windows and anyone outside. At first the Germans took cover, surprised by the attack, but in time became aware that the Polish attackers were few and not well-armed. The Luftwaffe men gathered their excellent supply of weapons and began planning a counterattack.

The German security building was attacked by Boleslaw Nowakowski. His armed men entered and ordered "hands up!" One Nazi officer, with a defiant expression stood arrogantly and refused. When he was shot dead, all remaining German hands, thus motivated, speedily reached for the sky.

At the "white church" of Saint Michael, Nazi SS men had been documenting some of the newly conscripted teenage boys. The SS men looked with alarm from behind the garden walls as shots rang out and a battle started in the town below. One of them loaded several rifles and began handing them out to the new recruits.

"Start shooting at those partisans down there!" the SS man bellowed.

The Polish boys, initially surprised and hesitant, just looked at each other until one gave a slight nod. They quickly turned the rifles on the hated SS men and fired, killing them from close range. Then, whooping with excitement, they ran off to join the fighting partisans.

Józef Niedźwiecki left the Jewish cemetery at the first bell. His first task was to cut the telephone lines heading to Minsk before attacking a gendarme security outpost. Józef sent his men ahead while he rode up to the place where the buried cables emerged from the ground and transitioned to hanging wires, suspended from pole to pole along the road. He dismounted with an ax and with several strikes broke the cables.

"HALT!" came the shocking order from a German soldier.
Where the hell did he come from? Józef thought to himself, as the soldier approached quickly, his rifle trained on Józef. *He must have been behind a nearby house.*

"Hands up!" came the next order as the German slowed his pace, stopping a few feet away. Just then a huge explosion sounded out and shook the ground. The German soldier instinctively jerked his gaze away and looked for the source of the blast, and the rifle dipped away with his movement. It was the bridge over the Wolma River being blown up by the partisans. The German returned his focus quickly, but Józef had his pistol out and was already firing.

Three quick shots dropped the soldier where he stood. Józef grabbed the soldier's rifle and ammo, mounted up and rode off to catch up with his men. He found them in the perfect position, just as planned, surrounding the security outpost. The three Nazis manning the building surrendered after receiving the shouted warning. The next task was to head to the gendarmerie and help with what was assumed to be an ongoing battle.

Jan Niedźwiecki was ecstatic, as the explosion signified that the radio station was destroyed, and this initial charge was a success. He hesitated, wondering if he should continue into the building or wait for the second wave of attackers. The backup should have arrived already but the timing had been thrown off by the early bell. The priest or brother responsible for the ringing had either had an out of sync clock or more likely had nervously panicked and just started early. *Opończa's* men had tried to pace themselves perfectly but were only then reaching the entrance and running up the walk.

Jan heard German voices shouting and heavy footsteps in the halls to the left. He snapped in a full magazine and aimed toward the expected charge. But across the room to the right a door opened slightly and Jan saw a blur of movement before the door slammed shut. A "potato masher" style German grenade clattered across the floor, hit a table leg, and spun to a stop just a few feet away. As Jan tried to quickly back out the entrance door the blast of heat, light and sound hit him.

Jan tumbled backwards out of the building, coming to rest head down and sprawled out at the bottom of the staircase. He felt the searing pain of several shrapnel wounds, but sensed that something more was very wrong. His shaking hand felt along his right side, and his fingertips dipped into the soft wetness of a large gaping wound. "Dear God," he whispered as his head started swimming.

On June 19, 1943, under the clear blue skies, so early in the battle that the church bells were still ringing, Jan Niedźwiecki bled out and died on the steps of the gendarmerie.

In 1943, in a town like Iwieniec, the ringing of the Angelus bells would have been a daily signal for the townsfolk to pause for a moment of prayer. On this particular day, the grenade blasts, artillery fire and shouting would have distracted many from this typical routine. Yet some others would have reacted to the chaos by praying even more fervently... *Święta Maryjo, Matko Boża, módl się za nami grzesznymi teraz i w godzinę śmierci naszej. Holy Mary, Mother of God, pray for us sinners, now and at the hour of our death.*

Meanwhile, as some were dying and others were praying, the Luftwaffe men dashed out of the barracks in coordinated groups, laying down suppressing fire as they leapfrogged from cover to cover, heading for the road. If they could break the encirclement they would escape down the road and link up with the garrison in Iwieniec. The combined forces would surely put down this uprising. With only small arms and sparse ammunition, the Poles were failing to hold up the well-armed and coordinated escape.

The first grouping of the Luftwaffe reached the road. But the Polish battle plan was sound. Hidden behind stone walls at the road entrance, Miłaszewski had set up two CKM machine gun units. When the first wave of Germans broke out they were hit from two angles by the withering fire of the powerful guns. Back and forth on the heavy tripods the guns swung, and a dozen of the enemy fell instantly. A few managed to escape and retreat, while several were forced to lay flat. The road was blocked. The trapped Germans, unable to move forward or back, were captured, and among them were two officers. This gave Miłaszewski an idea.

The meticulously planned objectives were being achieved all around Iwieniec. The surprise and careful coordination was working. The attack on the gendarmerie building was, by then, the main battle in town. Since the entrance assault had been repulsed by the grenade attack and the onrushing gendarmes, the next wave of men couldn't enter and were only able to grab Jan by the arms and drag his body back behind the berms. The large contingent of German soldiers had barricaded themselves in and were fighting back fiercely. They, like the Luftwaffe, also realized that they were better armed and could charge out and overwhelm the Poles.

The surrounding partisans were almost out of ammunition already, and were shooting sporadically and only when a clear shot appeared. A loss of containment here and the whole battle could be lost.

Miłaszewski dispatched a few men back to the gendarmerie with the captured German officer, who was sent out to order the gendarmes to surrender. The German walked forward and began shouting instructions when, inexplicably, he was gunned down by his compatriots from inside the building. Whether this was due to anger, or was some type of mistake is unknown, but the fight went on.

The gendarmes spotted a weak point in the Polish encirclement and quickly launched a counterattack to break out. Józef was riding hard to the battle with his men and saw *Lech* stand up and wave him toward the breakout. Józef instantly saw the situation and swerved his charging horse toward the danger, followed by his galloping men. They dismounted at the earthworks with a leap and pulled their weapons out just in time to slow the charge. But the lack of firepower was not enough to push the assault back to the building.

Just when the gendarmes started advancing again, weapons arrived from the cache seized at the Police station. Partisans ran up to the Polish lines with arms full of rifles and boxes of ammo and these were put instantly into use. The barrage of new gunfire turned the Germans back to the shelter of the building.

It was shortly after this turning point that Józef learned of his brother's death. The shock was great but he continued manning the earthworks and directing his men.

After several hours, the battle was won everywhere except the Luftwaffe barracks and the gendarmerie. The Luftwaffe fought into the night but could never manage to escape from the, by then, well supplied Polish encirclement.

The gendarmes were barricaded in with a large supply of ammunition and a stout building. The Poles could not dislodge them, so a stalemate of sporadic gunfire dragged on into the night.

Jan Jakubowski and Anton Kwiatkowski had been members of the fire brigade before the war and thought of a way to end the standoff. They dashed off to retrieve one of the pump trucks, filled its water tanks with petrol and drove it back to the battle. From a distance the truck slowly circled the gendarmerie building as the powerful pumps sprayed the fuel onto the walls and through the shot out windows. The ensuing conflagration, lit by fired rockets, took only seconds to engulf the building. The holed up German soldiers began running out, some with clothing on fire, and were cut down by the surrounding Polish guns.

The Iwieniec uprising was over. It was a stunning victory for the Polish partisans. Around the city Polish flags were unfurled and waved. Polish patriotic songs blared out from phonographs placed in windows, and citizens ran out into the streets with joyful faces.

The leaders gathered and took stock of the situation. They had only lost three men. Approximately one hundred and fifty enemy soldiers had been killed. The many Germans captured and disarmed early in the battle were being driven off to a distant town to be released where they could do no harm. Huge quantities of weapons and supplies were gained. The arrested Poles from the underground were successfully rescued, as well as several Jewish doctors and other Jewish citizens who had also been caught in the German net.

But no one had yet found Czech. The search continued but he had disappeared completely. When it came to actual fighting, this brazen killer had taken the coward's route, and hidden himself in a wood chip pile at the sawmill to wait out the battle.

The minute fighting ceased Józef let his grief pour out. He cried alone for a few moments then steeled himself. He had to be strong in front of his men. He had to go tell his family that their beloved, handsome, funny Jan was gone. Amid the ecstatic joy in the town he trudged back to his home. Everyone was celebrating and cheering around town, but when Józef walked by they went silent. The grief and sorrow in his face was so disturbing, and so understandable, that they turned away and did not look at him. There was nothing to be said.

Józef entered his home and immediately saw that the news had preceded him. Family members sat around the table sobbing or with blank, puffy faces. He pulled up a chair and sat down, staring off into space, listening to muffled cries.

"Where is Helena?" he eventually asked.

"She is laying down on her bed," replied Rufina.

Józef went in and sat on the edge of the bed. Helena briefly looked up and then turned away again, shutting her eyes tight. Józef placed his hand on her shoulder for a moment, then got up to leave. He heard her whisper.

"At least one of you is still alive."

He went back out to the main room. A fiery ember was starting to burn in his chest. Blame, anger and hatred joined the turmoil of his flooding emotions. There was one man most responsible for this tragedy, and Józef focused the intensity of his wrath on this figure. He stood silently in the room, swaying slightly with exhaustion, as his mind went to a dark place. He stared blankly. The total silence that suddenly blanketed the room snapped him out of his stupor, and he looked up. The whole family was staring at him with alarm. Obviously, his countenance had changed.

"So help me God, I am going to kill Czech!" he said.

As the Poles exulted in victory, and diligently followed the plans for the aftermath of the battle, Russian partisans galloped into town and announced that they were there to help. Despite being told the battle was over, the Russians still decided to stay and help themselves to as much German food and supplies as they could find.

The soldiers and many townspeople began mobilizing to leave town. They knew the Germans would get word of the uprising and respond with overwhelming force very soon. All the fighters planned to leave for the forest and all civilian helpers were urged to join them.

Eventually, a group of over six hundred were ready, having loaded their new supplies and important possessions into wagons and carts. At six in the morning two German reconnaissance planes were spotted circling around town. The time to leave was at hand.

Józef met with his family. Helena was joining the partisans and leaving with him. His father and other two sisters were staying. Rufina had been using a fake name and documents during the German occupation, and felt she could weather the storm. Father was too old for living in the woods.

The historic Hejnał bugle call signaled everyone to move out. As the column began snaking out of town heading for the forest, the crowds started singing. First the national anthem and then next a traditional song about the local region and its prominent river, the Niemen. The latter was a poetic accounting of a conversation between a soldier leaving for war and his love to be left behind.

The Russian partisans were still milling about, many were hungover from the previous night, having liberated Czech's substantial liquor supply. Cavalry commander Nurkiewicz warned them that the Germans were on the way, but they took little heed. The long column of Polish fighters, family members and others made their way deep into the Naliboki forest, traveling all day until reaching their first camp.

The captured supplies included two anti-tank cannons with ammo, two cars, three trucks, hundreds of grenades, hundreds of firearms including CKM and RKM machine guns, twelve thousand rounds of ammunition, many horses, food, medical supplies, boots, and some cattle.

A few hours later waves of German trucks and tanks rolled into Iwieniec. Hundreds of troops bounded off the trucks and quickly overran every part of town. The Polish partisans were long gone but many Russian partisans were caught and quickly killed.

Czech came out of hiding to meet the German forces. He was apoplectic with rage but also apprehensive of how he would be judged for the debacle. He somehow remained in charge of Iwieniec, suffering no demotion. With his active involvement, a hunt for rebels began. The Nazis would have their murderous reprisals, and as it turned out, a hundred dead civilians would be just the start. The religious brothers at

"Za Niemen"

"Beyond the Niemen, onward. The horse and arms are ready,
my girl, my love, give me an embrace, but give me my sword."

"Beyond the Niemen, beyond the Niemen,
why always beyond the Niemen?
Your heart is not there...
What is luring you beyond the Niemen?
Is the land more beautiful?
Are there more flowers in the meadows?
Are the girls so much prettier that you hurry there?"

" I am not hurrying to see more beautiful girls,
I am hurrying to drink the red honey of the unfaithful,
to spill the Muscovites blood."

"Then wait my darling, I will satisfy you, my chest is torn open,
so take my heart, drink my blood and fill yourself with my tears.
I can fill you."

"My darling stop, your words are like razors.
I will come back from the battlefield.
I will return because I am yours."

"My darling, you won't come back.
Your heart will withdraw, your memory will forget.
Look, your horse has already left his pasture and stall,
and on the red battlefield no doubt is your grave."

"But my God is great and I trust in my weapon,
and wherever I wield it the enemy will fall."

"Well if that is your will, to go to the battlefield
with such determination,
then heavy is my loss, and I am filled with terror.
I am going to pour out a flood of tears and prayers
to God that it be his will to protect you
and shield you from the enemy."

the monastery, known and beloved for their kindness and generosity to the locals, were all immediately lined up and shot because of their involvement in the bell ringing. Only Father Hilary, who was out on a sick call, escaped the bullets and managed to join the partisans in the forest. Many of the prominent underground families that chanced a stay were rounded up quickly and murdered.

A terrible story was relayed about how Czech and two henchmen arrived at the house of some underground members who had stayed in town. It was a couple weeks after the uprising and things seemed to have quieted down. Czech invited himself to dinner and sat with the terrified family while his armed men stood aside. He calmly ate and chatted until he had finished his meal. Then he folded up his napkin and set it aside, stood up and walked to the door before turning back and giving his men the signal. The soldiers lifted their weapons and machine-gunned the still seated family, killing them all.

The Soviet partisan leadership in the region noted the Iwieniec uprising with great alarm. They were shocked by the scale and success of the attack. They themselves had no similar accomplishment despite having thousands more soldiers in the region. And they had been completely left out of the Polish plans. Obviously, the Poles did not trust them, and wanted to assert their own independence in their own homeland. This could not stand.

On June 22, 1943, General Ponomarenko laid down a secret directive. A death sentence on all the local patriotic Polish partisans. This order explains the otherwise incomprehensible treachery of Soviet behavior in the region in the coming months.

The spectacular Iwieniec Uprising was one of the largest and most successful partisan battles of World War II. But because it took place in an area and a country that fell under the Soviet sphere of control, its story was repressed for many decades, and is still not widely known.

Chapter Nine

NALIBOKI FOREST – OPERATION HERMANN

THE PARTISANS AND the others had carefully worked their way down the trails, slogging through wetlands and dense woods, until they reached an area near Lake Kroman that was safe to set up camp. They built dug out houses, set up corrals for the horses, and began organized training. With plenty of supplies, including the cattle, kitchens were opened up. They gathered for meals and then often played cards afterwards, creating a community atmosphere. Learning the use and care of the highest quality German weaponry was a priority.

The death of Jan was devastating to Józef and Helena. But they were able to focus on service. Józef was put to use by cavalry commander Nurkiewicz for scouting expeditions throughout the forest. There were plenty of horses but few men ready for cavalry missions.

Helena learned to handle the new German weapons they had obtained, sitting at a table for hours loading and unloading ammo.

Zdzisław Nurkiewicz was experienced and highly decorated from both the 1919-1920 Polish-Soviet war and from the 1939 campaign. He had been standard bearer for the historic 27th cavalry regiment, and used his great organizational skills to start rebuilding this unit. Cavalry was the most difficult force to set up because of the need for support for the horses and because of the special skills required of its men and women.

Jan Jakubowski and Józef Niedźwiecki were soon singled out for leadership.

The partisans' purpose wasn't merely to train and build accommodations in the forest. Their purpose was to fight the invaders. Miłaszewski soon organized attacks on nearby German-allied Belarus police outposts, and broke them up in successful strikes.

It was not only the Russians that were shocked and alarmed by the uprising and the creation of a Polish partisan army. The Nazis were also planning an overpowering response. Reports began filtering in to the Polish Command that the Germans were building up troops in the vicinity, the first rumblings of an earthquake to come. Nurkiewicz and his budding cavalry platoons made it a priority to gather as much news as possible. What they found on reconnaissance was alarming. Huge numbers of equipment and troops seemed to be gathering near the edges of the Naliboki forest.

Miłaszewski made contacts with the Russians again. With such a lethal threat building, the combining of efforts could perhaps save both groups. Plans were approved to work together.

The German assault was called *"Operation Hermann"* and it was gigantic. The enemy command had decided to send a force of sixty thousand troops with trucks, tanks, and planes to totally pacify the region. No mercy would be shown, and even civilians would be brutalized and liquidated lest they provide future help to partisans.

On the 13th of July, 1943, Nurkiewicz reported huge columns of forces moving forward. The Poles set up two ambush points at the main roads and bridges that entered the forest. Because of the rugged and boggy terrain around them, the main entry points to the Naliboki forests were defensible. The newly acquired German CKM's, RKM's and anti-tank guns were hidden near the entry points, and the terrain prepared by cutting down trees into logjams to further stop advances. Two main bridges were blown up.

On the 20th of July, the ominous sound of marching was heard and the first Germans arrived at the entries. The blown bridges caused visible consternation as the observing Poles watched. Some German troops began crossing the swampy stream on foot, but sank to their hips in mud and struggled to either cross or retreat. That's when the Poles opened up with machine gun fusillades. Many of the enemy were stuck and dropped dead in the mud as others panicked to retreat.

The fleeing Germans scrambled back to take cover behind the cars and trucks, but the heavy Polish guns were next trained onto the vehicles. Tires and windows blew out and several vehicles exploded into flames. This first skirmish turned into a rout. The second bridge area entry attempt was also turned back by the Polish defense.

The next day the Germans launched an artillery barrage and sent in planes for strafing and bombing. They weren't going to be surprised again. The Poles continued cutting down trees and flooding ditches to slow the movements, but the Nazi forces slowly and painstakingly pushed forward. With such large numbers and devastating weapons, it was only a matter of time. Eventually some columns of tanks broke through and found areas of solid ground, clearing a path for the infantry following behind. They were in, spreading out, and ready to turn the forest into a bloodbath.

Miłaszewski planned a defensive stand to hold a line in concert with the Russians. Polish forces manned up the left flank bordering some bogs while the Russians guarded the right flank. As the Germans approached, Polish forward troops were able to disable two tanks, and then return to the lines. The armies met and the advance of the Germans slowed as the battle raged along the line. But something was immediately alarming to Polish commanders. Where was the sound of fighting to the right? The only awful sound seemed to be the loud engines of tanks and half-track trucks moving at steady speed. Miłaszewski hastily sent a scouting party to find out what was happening.

"Run, and get back fast", he ordered, "we need information now!" The scouts didn't have to go far to see what had occurred, and returned quickly and out of breath.

"The Russians have abandoned their positions, there is no one guarding the flank, we are about to be encircled."

Miłaszewski sprang into action. He sent the runners back down the line and ordered a fast, fighting retreat away from the advancing pincer movement. The Germans knew exactly what to do though, and picked up the pace on the edge while holding the middle. The Poles at the far end started dying in numbers as tank shells landed followed by infantry fire.

The fighting retreat fell apart as the overwhelmed partisans broke and ran. Only the rugged terrain saved the Poles from total disaster as the thick woods and intermittent boggy areas slowed down the tanks. The Poles lost many men before the remainder escaped back into the deep forest. Józef lost track of Helena at this time, as the partisans went on the run and were scattered.

The Germans soon controlled many of the main roads throughout the massive forest area. It became a hunt and destroy mission. Every small hamlet was entered and the population abused. The lucky were loaded on trucks and deported to slave labor in Germany. But brutal murder and cruelty were also the norm. Many villages were massacred, sometimes with all the men, women and children being herded into barns which were then set afire.

Included in the anti-partisan German units were such notorious war criminals like the SS Dirlewanger Brigade. Led by the monstrous and sadistic Oskar Dirlewanger, the unit was made up mostly of formerly imprisoned violent criminals, turned loose by the authorities to serve the Nazi cause. Dirlewanger, despite his imprisonment and seedy past, had patrons high up in the Nazi party. He was released and given a commission, where his foul band of reprobates had free rein over the innocent population.

The Polish partisans split up into smaller groups to try and escape the dragnets. Józef found himself with a band of several dozen moving along a low grassy dike between swamps. It was only wide enough for the wagons to travel single file, so they moved along slowly and carefully so as not to slide off the edges. When the sound of a plane was heard in the distance, the column tried to speed up to get off the narrow trail. But the plane spotted them and immediately circled in for strafing. It opened up with machine guns and they were trapped in a line of death. The horses panicked and leaped, carts of their hard earned weapons and supplies slid off the dike and dumped into the swamps. People were hit with hideously destructive bullet wounds to heads and torsos, sprawling off horses and carts and into the mud. The others leapt into the water to escape.

In just a few passes the destruction was unbelievable. The aftermath was a bloody scene of total mayhem. Many men and women were dead. Horses were killed, wounded, or stuck in the bogs up to their shoulders, entangled with wagons and harnesses. Józef and some others tried to take charge. They had to get the living back up and moving. Whatever weapons or supplies they could retrieve they gathered with haste. There was only one useable cart and horse left, on which they placed two injured partisans: one a teenage boy and the other a woman, but their wounds did not look good. The retreat from the dike commenced to the sound of muffled crying and despair.

They reached a dry area off the dike and rested. Józef had some fires built to dry clothes and warm up the survivors. The two injured had already died and were removed from the cart. There was no food.

After the brief rest, the bedraggled group moved on and eventually came to a small cottage where they found some other partisan survivors. They discussed their situation. Most had not eaten for four days. Almost all supplies were gone. But the forests were vast and it was still possible to hide out and avoid the Germans. Most of the group wanted to stay put in this hideout. Despite no prospect of food they desperately needed rest. Many had lost their footwear and had bloody, injured feet.

"I am going to scout around," Józef said. "Maybe I can link up with some others or maybe find some food." He went out and unharnessed the horse from the cart, mounted up, and headed out. He did not mention his desperate hope to also find Helena.

Józef traveled carefully, stopping every little while to listen intently. He did not want to stumble into a German patrol or camp. It was difficult finding trails through the bogs and rivulets, but that also meant it was not ideal for the mechanized enemy. He found some higher ground and passed through a wooded area of giant ancient trees. Józef recognized the terrain. It was an area that he had camped in as a boy, and he looked for an old trail.

There should be a boy scout lodge at the end of this tract, he remembered. The old structure eventually came into sight, and Józef was pleased to see some Poles occupying the camp and the small meadow. There, much to his surprise, he found Miłaszewski and some cavalry members. Miłaszewski gave him a brief smile before his face returned to grave seriousness.

"I see you have managed to stay alive... that's good... do you want some food?"

They sat down to a small plate of boiled potatoes and discussed the situation. Miłaszewski pulled out maps and spread them out. He described where he thought the German concentrations were and where he thought some of their partisans were hiding out.

Miłaszewski went on, "We have lost a lot of our members, many were killed, many were captured. I want to try to save who we can, so we have to actively work to find them and bring them to safe areas. The whole region is blockaded in. Eventually, we may find some ways to escape from it, if we can make it to an edge of the forest, but right now it's a matter of surviving one day at a time."

He sent Józef out the next day to search for survivors, and depending on where he found them, to take them to the safest areas based on the maps. Other members of the cavalry were sent out on the same mission. Józef showed Miłaszewski where he left the group at the cottage, so that food could be sent to them.

Józef rode through a fire-ravaged hamlet the first day. It looked like the inhabitants were all shipped out, except for several corpses that were left scattered in the fields. He dismounted and approached the remnants of a barn that was still smoldering. As he walked up towards the charred beams and timbers, he thought he saw something in the blackened debris. The hair stood up on his arms and a terrible feeling overcame him. Slowly, he backed away without looking closer, and went back to his horse. He avoided lingering at the terrible place and moved on quickly.

Some distance down the trail Józef heard the sound of an engine, and changed course to give a wide berth. He found some fresh sets of horse tracks and followed them. After hours of careful tracking, he spotted movement ahead and dismounted to peer through the trees.

Through the shifting forest light and swaying branches a familiar sight emerged: Polish uniform caps. Józef quickly mounted his horse and rode up to greet them. They now had a group of four to continue the search.

The next day was unsuccessful, but the following day they found a group of stragglers hiding out in deep undergrowth. They were in terrible shape: starving, weak, with clothes ripped to shreds from hiking through brush. The group took turns either riding double or walking, until they arrived at an emptied village. There was shelter, and abandoned food to scrounge up, so they all stayed for a day. However, the next day Józef and his riders moved on. The men spotted several runaway horses grazing together and gathered them up to bring along.

In a week the group had found dozens of partisan survivors, brought them to safe areas, and outfitted a small cavalry unit of men with the extra horses. It was the nucleus of what would become Józef's own 2nd squadron of the cavalry.

Operation Hermann was still in full swing though, and the odds of survival looked bleak. In each safe area, Józef directed his men to post lookouts for signs of approaching enemy. He also had them form contingency plans in case there was sudden need to escape and hide. His little cavalry unit only had four rifles and two pistols for the nine men, so they were focused solely on survival at this point, and not fighting.

The depopulated and partially burned out hamlets and homesteads were providing enough food and shelter for the starving partisans and other inhabitants to survive. One would find a place with a few chickens or other livestock milling about, some vegetable gardens undamaged, and occasionally some surviving pantries of food stock.

It was at one such place that Józef finally heard the news he had hoped for. A group of fellow partisans rode in and reported that a few kilometers away there was another group of survivors that included Helena. Overjoyed, Józef asked one of his men to take an extra horse and bring her to join his growing camp, while he continued organizing the increasing numbers of survivors.

He selected "*Bohun*," who was proving to be a reliable and trusted soldier. He was older than most of the men, and his maturity impressed Józef.

For almost a week they had avoided German patrols, but this day their luck ran out. Shortly after *Bohun* left on his task, a German reconnaissance plane buzzed the camp. They were spotted. Immediately the escape plan went into action. The SS would move fast, using whatever roads were available to get close to the area and then hunt them down. The partisans split into three groups and headed out on pre-planned routes. Those on foot took to small trails into the bogs, snaking their way into dense thickets that no vehicle or horse could follow. Józef took his mounted troop down a dry trail and then split off into the woods. They would draw attention away but hopefully move fast enough to lose their trackers.

As Józef sped through the forest, he realized that having finally found his sister, he had set her up to walk right into the clutches of Nazi killers. *God keep her safe*, he prayed.

For most of the day, Józef's riders kept moving, winding down trails and changing course frequently, making sure to not accidentally circle back toward the hunters. A plane occasionally flew near, looking for them. They didn't know if it spotted them. A few hours later they heard mechanized sounds again, but up ahead, on some distant road. Then, to their shock, they heard voices and horses approaching. The Germans were in close pursuit.

"We are not going to outrun them anymore" Józef told his men. He was thinking hard, trying to formulate a plan for escape. They all paused, watching him closely. He took several minutes in deep concentration.

"We are going to surprise them," he said. "Give them a tiny taste of being the prey, and buy enough time to get away. Follow me."

He quietly set off on a trot, starting a path that would circle them around. Twenty minutes later he had them dismount and tie off the horses. They could just barely hear the sound of the enemy approaching.

"Listen carefully," Józef instructed, "don't make a sound once we start. We are going to walk up to an ambush point, I will direct you where to go. There will probably be one or two scouts in the lead, tracking us. We will try to take them out. Whether we hit them or miss they will still take cover and hunker down for some time. We will be long gone, hopefully, before they realize it."

Józef paused and searched the attentive faces. "Anatol will take the first shot. Kaz will take the second. All of you will leave right after that second shot, unless heavy fighting breaks out. Get back to the horses and head back the way we came, until you reach the canal. Then circle around it, and we will meet up at that pine grove where we can hide from planes until the pressure eases."

A few of the men glanced back over their shoulders. The Germans were getting closer. Józef lowered his voice. "I will take the third shot and maybe more, depending on how they react. I will follow shortly, but I am going to swim across the canal rather than circle it, which will confuse their trail. They won't be swimming, and will probably give up at dusk... ready?"

The men nodded in affirmation.

They followed single file as Józef snuck up on the approaching Germans. He found an area of slightly higher ground above the trail they had previously followed, the trail the Germans were then tracking. They could hear them coming. Józef pointed out locations for each man to lie prone, picking good sight lines for the shooters.

The first sight of a Nazi helmet appeared, bobbing in the distance, appearing and disappearing between the leafy saplings in the sun dappled woods. Then a second soldier. The two scouts were talking quietly together as they moved steadily along. Józef put his hand up to alert Anatol, who adjusted his rifle into a ready position and peered sideways at Józef, waiting.

The lead scout passed Józef, who was first along the line. When the rider was directly below Anatol, Józef gave the signal. Anatol hesitated until the rider was fully visible in a gap opened between tree trunks, then fired. A gasp sounded out and the rider slumped off his horse to the ground. Kaz fired his shot as shouting erupted below. The Germans were quickly dismounting and taking cover behind any tree, log, or rock they could get behind. Józef was aware of his men leaving as he looked for a target. Every German was hiding. Far to the back of the line he spotted an aggressive soldier, crouched down but aiming his carbine at the ridgeline, trying to find the Polish shooters. Józef sighted in and fired, and heard the sound of glancing metal, followed by someone below swearing loudly in German. Józef decided to empty out some more rounds into the trees below, splintering branches among the pinned down enemy. Then he crawled backwards, got up, and in a crouching run took off through the trees.

Once out of sight he ran hard. In minutes he was back to his horse and riding off. Józef reached the canal as the sun was just starting to dip below the tree tops. The canal was large and wide, definitely not swimmable in clothes and boots, but that wasn't the plan.

He got off his horse and listened carefully for his pursuers. Nothing. He took his rifle and ammo pouch and tied them to the saddle, then guided the hesitant horse into the water. When it was fully in he grabbed hold and urged it on. It cleared bottom and began swimming across, dragging him nicely behind. When they reached the opposite shore his horse smartly chose a good landing spot and clambered out immediately. As the evening shadows grew, he rode off toward the rendezvous.

It was a day later and in a new hiding spot that news of Helena finally reached Józef's agonizing wait. But it wasn't what he had hoped for. *Bohun* arrived at the new camp alone.

He was covered in mud and dirt and looked exhausted, limping in without a horse. Józef ran out to him.

"Where is Helena?" he demanded.

"I left her in the woods," *Bohun* stated.

"You left my sister in the woods?" Józef repeated, not comprehending.

"I hid her and her friend, and barely escaped myself."

Bohun recounted the story. He had found Helena as ordered, and she was ecstatic to rejoin her brother. She had her close friend Barbara with her, and they both wanted to stay together, so *Bohun* agreed to bring them both back with him the next day. Helena and Barbara rode double on the extra horse and happily headed out for the ride to Józef's camp. They had no idea that the camp was already being assaulted by German troops.

"We walked right into sight of an SS unit." *Bohun* recounted.

Once spotted they turned their horses and made a run for it, heading into the boggy areas as their best chance. The Germans tracked them for hours. They managed to stay just far enough ahead to elude capture, but then both horses sank into swampy mud and were stuck. They had to abandon the horses and set off on foot.

For several more hours they struggled along, but couldn't manage to put enough distance between themselves and the SS unit.

"They seemed to be everywhere, front, back, sides, every direction we went."

The three Poles were sinking up to their knees in mud. Eventually the exhausted girls couldn't go on.

"We had to take a chance, or just give up completely."

They found a small patch of drier ground with a mossy carpet growing on it.

"I did the old scout trick and peeled back the moss... we scratched the peat out with our hands, and I hid the girls under a moss carpet. Then I continued on, hoping to draw the trackers away and escape to reach you. I told them to hold out until night, when I would return with you to guide them out of the woods. The Germans don't venture into the swamps at night."

"Go sleep for a couple hours. At sunset we head out for them." Józef ordered.

They set out as planned. It was a dark night and the trails were hardly visible. They stepped off into deep wet mud frequently and hit patches of thorny brush. It seemed an impossible task. *Bohun* tried to backtrack his previous journey, but the swamps, difficult to navigate during daylight, at night just looked like repetitive reflections of water and endless trees. They started losing hope. Eventually they were deep into the swamps and Józef began wondering if they would be lost until morning. Despair set upon him. *My sister*, he said softly to himself. The area would be swarming with Germans again the next day, and the girls' odds of evading capture for another day were slim. Helena and Barbara didn't know which direction to head.

Bohun thought he was in the right area, but couldn't be sure. The two men sat down on a log and rested for a moment. Józef heard a faint sound, different from the insects and amphibian sounds that are a constant din in swampy areas. He was suddenly alert.

"What was that noise?" he asked.

"Didn't hear it," said *Bohun*.

A few minutes later they both heard the short shrill sound.

"A bird?" *Bohun* asked.

They waited. A few minutes later it sounded out again, very distant. Józef was on his feet now, standing very still. He had to identify this sound. It was so very faint, yet a spark of hope had fired up in his brain.

"Did you hear it?" he asked. He had to get closer, so slogged in the direction as fast as possible, *Bohun* right behind. After another pause, they heard it again, this time louder and recognizable, and Józef's wildest and most unlikely hope exploded in an epiphany.

"It's Helena!" Józef shouted out. "It's her whistle!"

He sprang forward immediately, moving desperately towards the sound. *Bohun* followed.

Józef crashed through brush and staggered through mud for several strenuous minutes, then halted to listen. The next blast came, a bit clearer, and Józef struggled forward again as fast as possible. With each burst of progress the sound became louder. The intervals were very consistent.

Józef forged ahead, regardless of terrain, sometimes walking through knee-deep water. His face was getting whipped by branches he could not see in the darkness, and *Bohun* followed right behind. They were getting so close that *Bohun* realized how loud the whistles actually were. They had come a long, long distance.

"Helena!" Józef finally shouted out, when he thought it could be heard.

"Here!" came back the beautiful, familiar voice.

Helena later described in detail her scary ordeal. After *Bohun* left, the girls lay still, concealed under their moss blankets. A German troop actually walked right by Helena's hiding spot. She was absolutely sure they would hear her heart beating in her chest, as it seemed so alarmingly loud to her. It was several minutes of pure terror. The Germans eventually moved on, but the girls stayed hidden all day until dark, when the woods quieted down.

Helena fully trusted that her brother would come for her, and thought of starting the intermittent whistle late in the evening. Once reunited, the four partisans somehow found a good horse trail in the darkness and made it out of the bogs before dawn.

As the days wore on, the German project of emptying hamlets by murdering or deporting the residents continued. Once this was largely accomplished the German soldiers focused more and more on hunting down partisans. Former poachers released from prison aided groups like the Dirlewanger Brigade in tracking and hunting people.

Józef had by then gathered a large group of mounted men and women, and after many days on the run had reached an area near the edge of the Naliboki forest. There was a chance to save his too-easily trackable group by breaking out of the blockade. They headed south and scouted the exit points of the Naliboki forest, looking for a lightly watched area. All roads leading out were guarded and most of the unguarded areas in between were wetlands. Scouts were sent out and they finally found a fast and clear trail, but it was within sight to the east of a heavily guarded crossroads, where the Germans had cleared everyone out and taken over the cluster of buildings. Józef decided they would attempt a diversion and a breakout in the dark of night.

On the evening of the plan the partisans rode out and split into two groups. The larger first group headed to the woodland trail, giving the German command post a wide berth and staying hidden. Then they waited. Józef led the smaller diversion team, made up of just a few men. They headed toward the crossroads held by the Germans, and then dismounted. From this point they moved quietly on foot until they reached some unguarded outbuildings on the far end, away from the occupied buildings. In a small rickety barn they piled old hay into a corner and started a fire. Then they quickly retreated as the flames started to engulf the dry old structure. As they ran off they heard shouting. According to the plan, the rising fire was drawing attention away from the partisan escape route.

The waiting Poles rushed down the trail as soon as they saw the flames. The troop exited the woods, riding at full speed toward the road and away from the German camp. A short distance later they started crossing a field towards another tract of woods further south.

Józef and the diversion team exited a few moments later, just as the first group was spotted by the Germans. Before Józef's team turned onto the road they saw headlights flash, as soldiers hurried into vehicles to chase them down. But the partisans on horseback crossed the field too far ahead and the vehicles could only stop on the road and fire some shots from a distance. In the woods the whole troop merged and kept moving south. In the morning they changed course and headed to a small town well outside the blockade zone and hid out with friendly civilians.

Operation Hermann ended on August 13, 1943. The German units withdrew leaving devastation behind. Over sixty villages were completely destroyed. At least four thousand civilians were murdered, and twenty thousand shipped off for forced labor.

The six hundred Polish partisans from the Stołpce-Naliboki group, so well equipped and confident after the Iwieniec uprising, lost at least one hundred twenty, either killed or missing, and were down to a fighting force of approximately half their former strength. They lost most of their weapons and supplies. But they were still alive, and ready to rebuild.

Chapter Ten

Rebuilding

WEEKS LATER, JÓZEF NIEDŹWIECKI rode up and dismounted at Kacper Miłaszewski's headquarters. Inside the cottage, Miłaszewski sat with several staff and another officer that Józef didn't know. They were immediately introduced.

"This is Captain Adolf Pilch, who has been assigned to us," explained Miłaszewski.

Józef sized up the new man as they firmly shook hands. Pilch was stocky but fit looking. He had a confident air and a direct gaze. There was something in the way both Miłaszewski and Pilch were looking at him that Józef could not quite interpret.

Miłaszewski discussed Józef's orders for the next few days. The partisans had come out of *Operation Hermann* badly damaged. They were in the process of recovering, rearming, and rebuilding up the unit. There was a lot of work to do. Józef would continue as a cavalry leader under the experienced Warrant Officer Zdzisław Nurkiewicz.

The hope was to build up these units into a strong and well trained force. The whole partisan army, in fact, was being reorganized at a high level.

"One more thing," Miłaszewski started, after orders were finished. "Some of your men came to visit me," he said. Józef was surprised by this unexpected statement.

"They have asked to remain under your command, going forward. They were quite adamant, I have to say," Miłaszewski furthered, with an almost bemused expression on his face. Pilch had a slight smile at this also.

"I... uh... they are good men," Józef stammered out awkwardly.

Pilch chimed in, "They seem to be ready to follow you anywhere."

Miłaszewski started speaking again, but with a more serious tone. "They gave some detailed reports on your leadership, which we had already heard about of course. We are recommending you for the Medal of Valor, for your actions during the German operation. Congratulations."

Józef soon found out more about the mysterious new arrival Adolf Pilch. Pilch had fought with the Polish Army in France during the early part of the war. Later he ended up in England with Polish special forces. A Polish division of the English SOE (Special Operations Executive) formed a top secret and specialized paratrooper unit. This elite unit had over twenty-six hundred volunteers, of which only six hundred and six completed the strenuous training. Of those, just three hundred and sixteen operatives were eventually parachuted into occupied territory.

The physical and mental training was extreme. They learned every type of weapon from every country. They learned bomb making, topography, Jujitsu and sharpshooting. They practiced silent killing techniques and the art of shooting at invisible targets. Various local dialects and customs were taught. Everything a covert operative would need for partisan warfare. They hiked and ran twenty kilometers at a time.

These special forces became known as the *"Cichociemni"*, which translates roughly as the *"silent and unseen."* The name started out as a nickname, describing how the selected volunteers would suddenly disappear from their units during the night, but it became the official name for them, aptly describing their methods and operations. Pilch had parachuted into occupied Poland in February 1943 and arrived at the Stołpce - Naliboki group that summer.

The partisans got back to business. One of their initial goals was to again establish a counterforce to the large numbers of Russian partisans, who were still frequently abusing the local population with theft, violence and even murder. The protection of the civilians began anew. The Poles also resumed actions against the Nazi occupiers. The German garrisons at Duniłowicze and Zodziski were successfully attacked, gaining a much needed supply of new weapons.

The forest areas and remote villages became deadly for German activity. Any small unit heading out to requisition food or goods was at great risk of partisan ambush. The partisans owned the woods, and the Germans were forced to stick to the towns where they were less likely to be surprised by guerrilla attacks. The eastern front was rapidly turning disastrous for the Nazis. Given their losses at the front, the huge *Operation Hermann* looked like one of many tactical blunders, and the Germans could no longer afford to set aside sixty thousand troops for a pacification exercise. Despite the huge toll in human suffering, the aftermath found the Polish population to be even more motivated and resolute against the occupiers than before. The partisans had many new volunteers stream in, and received help from the locals like never before. They were supplied food and shelter with no request for payment from the friendly population.

During the summer Aleksander Warakomski, known as simply *"Swir"*, the regional commander, was a frequent visitor. He eventually made the decision that Adolf Pilch would be taking over as commander of the whole Stołpce-Naliboki group. Pilch was shocked and initially had reservations. He was only twenty-nine years old, and still pretty new to this group. But *Swir* saw a unique talent in Pilch and insisted. Miłaszewski became second in command. It could be seen as a demotion for Miłaszewski, which was a surprise to the men, as he had proven to be a popular and good leader. The thinking is that perhaps *Swir* felt Miłaszewski had acted too independently, not clearing major actions with the chain of command. The Iwieniec uprising in particular had been very secretive and locally carried out.

As it turned out, Pilch's brilliant leadership through the disasters and successes ahead became legendary. No partisan leader of World War II was his equal.

The Home Army held Masses frequently, whether in the woods or in available chapels. One of the priest chaplains, Father Mieczysław Suwała, described one of his own memories from that time:

"One Saturday evening in September, I sat on a stump in front of a long line of soldiers with weapons in hand. They approached me and knelt on one knee. I heard their confessions until late in the night. On Sunday morning, the unit formed a square, fully armed, in front of the altar. Dressed in Mass vestments with a chalice in my hands, I stood on the steps of the altar under the green spruce trees. The first Holy Mass in a partisan camp for me had begun. One of the soldiers started singing the *'Anthem of the Home Army.'* I cannot adequately describe this Mass for which the Naliboki Forest was the most beautiful green temple, gilded with the rays of the morning sun, and with the branches of the spruce trees forming the most beautiful canopy. I cannot describe the moment I held the Sacred Host most high, almost touching the boughs, over the heads of the kneeling soldiers, and the moment the soldiers received Holy Communion, almost in combat formation. After Mass, I went down to the foot of the altar. I said prayers for the fallen, then began singing 'God save Poland.' Five hundred partisans sang the refrain. The heart of the forest, maybe for the first time, heard the Mass and witnessed the prayers of the Polish partisans."

Translated lyrics to these beautiful and moving melodies are included on the following pages.

In the evenings the partisans often gathered for bonfires and singing. There is a rich tradition of Polish patriotic and partisan songs, as well as folk songs and Christian hymns. The feeling that they were all one big family grew. Some members had musical instruments to add to the scene. Józef had been in the KOP orchestra before the war and could play clarinet and accordion, so when someone delivered an accordion to the group, Józef added his talents. This soon became a favorite request because Józef had a good ear for music. He could make the instrument sound cheerful and energizing or plaintive and sorrowful, which was especially moving when heard deep in the woods by a campfire at night. When the group lost a member especially, singing one of the songs about sacrifice and struggle and missing loved ones brought tears to everyone's eyes. In his notes, Józef states that singing was the "cement" that brought everyone close together.

For Józef and Helena, a difficult but needed part of the grieving process over their beloved brother was playing and singing the song, *"Rozkwitały Pąki Białych Róż", or "White Roses."* This was a popular song among the partisans, and they couldn't hear the words without thinking of Jan.

Anthem of the Home Army
Modlitwa obozowa

"O Lord who art in heaven,
Extend the palm of your just hand,
We call to you from foreign lands,
We long for the shelter of our Polish home,
Oh God, shatter the sword that
slashed our homeland,
We long for the chance to take up arms.

Grant that we may return to a Poland
that is free,
To stand as a fortress of new strength.
Our home, our home.
Oh Lord, hear our lamentations,
hear the sound of our homeless song.

From behind the Warta,
the Wisła,
the San,
and the Bug,
The blood of our martyrs call to you."

God Save Poland
Boże Coś Polskę
(Translation of the Rev. Thos. Grochowski, C.Ss.R.)

God who hast compassed for so many ages
Poland with splendor of glory and power;
Whose shield almighty oft saved her in stages,
When dangers threatened her ruinous hour.

(refrain)
Unto thy altars we bring supplication,
Country and Freedom Lord restore our Nation!

It is not long since her Freedom was taken.
But our blood has been shed, deep as a river.
Oh, how unhappy, the people forsaken,
Who are deprived of their country forever!

God Thy just arm can break scepters of iron
Of Earth's bold rulers all power defying.
Crush the designs, that our foemen rely on;
Rouse in our Polish souls hopes never dying.

Oh God most holy! By Thy mighty wonder
Free us from warfare and murd'rous oppression,
Join all Thy nations in freedom's bonds under
One scepter of Peace in Thy angel's possession.

Lord of all sovereigns of Earth! Though art able
Out of the dust, by one word, to uplift us,
And Thou can'st punish our fealty unstable,
Turn us to dust but as FREE dust yet sift us!

White Roses
Rozkwitały Pąki Białych Róż

Come back from the war Johnny, come back,
Come back, kiss me like you did in the past,
When you do, I will give you one of these white roses,
For this, I give you a rose, the most beautiful flower.

The summer has passed, the fall, and now it's winter,
The rose has since stopped blooming,
What then, Johnny, will I give you,
When you return from the war to the one who loves you?

On an empty battlefield, a cold winter wind blows,
Beloved Johnny will never return,
Cruel death takes a bloody toll,
They buried your Johnny in a dark grave.

Johnny no longer needs my white roses,
White roses are with him still,
He lies buried beneath the mound
On which the buds of white roses
Have burst into bloom.

Don't despair my beloved,
It is not a tragic end,
To be buried under Polish soil,
Where our hardships
And sacrifice are never forgotten.

Chapter Eleven

MEDIC

JÓZEF HEARD THAT a teenage medic that had been with the partisans was resting at a house nearby, recovering from injuries he received during *Operation Hermann*. His name was Jan Kuzminski, and his mother was already serving as a nurse with the underground army. Jan had been trained by doctors in the Iwieniec hospital.

Józef arrived and found the boy looking comfortable and relaxed, laying on his back in a bed.

"My name is Sergeant Gray," Józef said, before asking, "What are you doing and why are you not back serving?"

"My feet are badly injured," replied Jan.

"I am taking a look." Józef unraveled the bandages and noted serious wounds to the bottom of the boy's feet.

"Ok, but don't let me see you walking around town before rejoining us. We need medics, my unit doesn't have even one. Remember, we partisans don't joke around."

"I am eager to get back, actually, as soon as I can walk," answered the boy, very earnestly.

Józef recognized him as one of three soldiers he had seen being disciplined in camp early on, before the German attack. The three teenagers had taken some jars of jelly and other supplies from a civilian who they suspected of being sympathetic to the Germans. The three walked in with guns drawn and demanded the man turn over the sought after goods. Then they ran to the woods and enjoyed their purloined delicacies.

It turned out that the man was operating as a double agent, secretly working for the Poles. Nevertheless, regardless of status, requisitioning anything from civilians without orders was strictly forbidden, and the young men were ordered to stand at attention with full backpacks and full dress for many hours in the hot sun as punishment. One eventually passed out, signaling the end of the exercise.

Jan Kuzminski had a reputation for being a comically impulsive and somewhat reckless young man. But this was more than made up for by his increasingly stellar abilities as a medic and his incredible dedication and bravery. By the end of the war he was known to be a true hero. He recovered from his foot injuries and served the partisans for the remainder of the group's activities together.

Chapter Twelve

Soviet Storm Clouds

Occasional meetings were still taking place with the Soviets. The goal of helping each other against the common enemy remained an elusive proposition. Suspicions dominated and recurrent bad behavior by Red partisans angered the Poles. Stories of robberies and rapes continued to filter in.

Kacper Miłaszewski was the main negotiator because of his perfect Russian. He was also smart and level headed, not susceptible to falling for bad faith tactics. Unfortunately, not all of Polish leadership proved to be as reticent and wise when arriving from other regions. The local Poles certainly continued to get warning signs that the Soviet intentions were self-serving.

Around this time some NKVD agents secretly approached warrant officer Zdzisław Nurkiewicz. His great experience, strong leadership, and success in building a cavalry had been noticed. They proposed he abandon the Poles and join the Communist Reds. For this move he would have all the men and horses he needed.

Nurkiewicz, the true patriot, was insulted and indignant. He gave them a very clear reply. He stood up, looked at the men fiercely and said, "I would rather spend my remaining days cleaning the boots of a Polish major, than be a Soviet one."

The insulted Russians rode off. A week later the same group approached Nurkiewicz's second in command, Jan Jakubowski, with a similar offer, but with a creative twist. He would have to assassinate Nurkiewicz first, before coming over. This was also emphatically declined.

At one point Józef was sent to meet with members of the Soviet *"Frunze Brigade"* to relay some messages and discuss unified strategy, but also to have a friendly meeting so as to gather any intelligence possible. He headed over with gifts of food and vodka and brought a good translator, even though most Poles and Russians in this region could communicate fairly well. After passing on some letters several of them sat down to eat. They were pleased to open the good vodka as they were down to local moonshine in their supply.

Józef had traveled under his *nom-de-guerre*, Sergeant *"Gray"*, in order to protect his real identity. He brought along the accordion which everyone enjoyed. He stayed for two days doing business in the mornings and drinking in the evenings, mindful to keep his wits at all times. The meeting was cordial and cheerful as the men found some common ground talking and laughing and singing some shared folk songs they all knew. Józef was able to hear some interesting stories as the drinking loosened everyone up.

They heard some riders approach on the second evening and the unit's NKVD officer walked in for the first time. The mood changed abruptly. The conversation trailed off and went stale. The officer must have noticed but appeared nonplussed, perhaps enjoying the fear he elicited. He began staring at Józef intently and was soon the one asking questions. Józef planned to make an exit as soon as possible. The party was definitely over. Józef spoke for a while longer about German movements and how they should split up certain territories.

"All this territory is Russian," the NKVD man said coldly, surprising Józef.

No one spoke for a moment of awkward silence, but Józef was boiling over inside, and tried to keep his cool. He decided to stay silent except to stand up and announce his departure, as it was well after dark.

"Will we see you again, Sergeant Gray?" asked the NKVD man.

"Perhaps, but I am pretty elusive," Józef answered, trying to make a joke and lighten the mood.

"We probably will," said the officer, "the Russians are good hunters, we can track a bear through the forest." This remark was lost on everyone else but not Józef, whose blood had turned to ice water. The name Niedźwiecki is derived from the word "bear".

Józef rode away. He was shocked that the NKVD agent obviously knew his true identity and gave him the threat. Clearly the officer was unhappy with Józef's fact finding mission and had warned him off.

He gave his angry report to Miłaszewski and Pilch, who were also alarmed about the "bear" remark and what that meant about Russian spying. Józef decided to speak freely with his strong opinions laid bare.

"They are a poor fighting force," Józef started, "because they are frequently drunk. They have mistresses they drag along, and the officers fight over them and over goods they steal. They have lost members due to squabbles and infighting, both to desertion and to drunken shootouts among themselves. They are paranoid of outsiders. Even medical treatment arouses suspicion, as they fear that doctors could be German spies that will poison them. The leadership is lazy, so they avoid fighting. Only the NKVD agents being sent in are pushing actions and creating any discipline. The rank and file soldiers still have a spark of humanity, but are so weakened morally that they cannot be trusted in any circumstance. I am confirming what we already have been aware of."

"Yes, Sergeant Gray," agreed Miłaszewski, "your report does confirm my own observations. I think about the mentality of the Soviets a lot also."

"They are not like us," finished Józef.

Pilch and Miłaszewski later gave a speech to the partisans about the different morality and behavior of their enemies. Pilch described a recent local incident.

A Russian unit had recently abducted two Polish girls to cook for their camp. The girls were abused at night by the officers. On the second day of captivity the girls waited until the inevitable drunken slumber overtook the Russian partisans. They slipped away, but did not run home. They went to the nearest German headquarters and angrily reported the location of the Russians and their present state of inebriation.

The Germans sent a kill team out instantly, found the Red unit as described, and liquidated every last member without a fight.

Pilch warned his men that in the current situation of war, a momentary lack of judgment or lack of self-discipline could mean a quick death. They had survived so much already, and the two leaders emphasized how proud they were of everyone for their faithfulness and dedication. They should continue to focus on abstinence and careful behavior. Staying alive was the first and foremost step in the fight against the invaders.

Chapter Thirteen

First Injury

JÓZEF CONTINUED TO ENJOY the great talents and abilities of former scouts among his men. They stepped into their roles as partisan fighters seamlessly. The town and city volunteers who hadn't scouted were a different story. They were just as brave and patriotic as the country boys, but did not have the skills or the overall sense of those who had spent time active outdoors.

As Józef trained them he emphasized the importance of constant vigilance and awareness of their surroundings. *Where could danger come from? Where is an escape route? Where is a hiding spot?* He was constantly asking them to refrain from excessive noise while in the field, and from otherwise making their presence known. It was a continual frustration and he hoped he could drill enough into them to prevent any unnecessary mishap.

On September 22nd, 1943 Józef was out scouting with his men. A group of newer volunteers had gone far ahead, and when Józef caught up with them, what he saw infuriated him. The forward group had stopped to rest in the middle of a large meadow, completely open and visible from the surrounding woodlands. Józef lost his cool, and immediately rode out to admonish them. He was thinking of the proper swear words and subsequent punishment when the machine guns opened up on them.

Józef's horse leaped and almost bucked him off, but he regained control and galloped towards his men, yelling to head for the far woods. The shocked partisans mounted up and tried to ride off quickly. To the side, Józef could see the flashes of two guns firing. Probably CKMs from the volume of fire. He caught a glimpse of a partially obscured vehicle, and then the men in German uniforms who had quickly set up for an attack after spotting the oblivious partisans. They were quite far off, luckily, or his forward group would all have been killed.

As Józef turned away he saw that one of his men was blood stained and barely hanging on to his ride. The others were reaching the woodline. A sharp pain, like being stabbed, jolted his hand. He reached the woods and darted between trees until catching up with the others. He had left the other part of his unit at the other woodline when he entered the meadow. They were mostly his experienced men though, so would probably make the right moves.

He looked at his pained hand and was thrown into shock. It was ripped open at the palm and gushing blood. He slid off the horse and called out for a medical kit. The real pain was coming by then, as his man wrapped it tight. The other injured man had a bullet wound to the back. Józef ordered his evacuation back to camp immediately. The soldier was still able to ride, so two men escorted him and left.

The machine gun fire had stopped when the partisans disappeared into the woods. But as they were attending Józef's medical situation gunfire erupted again, different this time, and then a grenade explosion echoed across the meadow. It went quiet again.

"Take the binoculars and see what's going on" Józef ordered, and one of his men jumped to it.

He reported back. "I can see our men skirting the edge of the meadow and heading this way."

They didn't have to wait long before the men rode up and gave Józef their own account:

"We circled behind them and wiped them out, the grenade finished them off. Killed seven. Three of our men are driving back the vehicle and the one undamaged CKM. What the hell! Look at your hand."

"That was a damn good job," said Józef. "I am proud of all of you. Yeah, my hand is shot up."

The camp doctor examined Józef's injury. He cleaned it out and felt for broken bones, then stitched it, splinted it, and wrapped it again.

"It's pretty bad, you may lose some use of it, you may not," the doctor explained. "You have to rest it completely without movement for at least a week. Once the open wounds heal you will have to try exercising it, which will be very painful. Drink vodka for the pain, it's all we have."

Józef was sent by Pilch to stay with some civilians, to ensure he would rest properly. He was in quite a lot of pain, but otherwise enjoyed the comfortable accommodations and good food. The family treated him like royalty. They had two teenage daughters who doted on him. He heard them whisper and giggle in the kitchen about "our blue eyed cavalry officer."

Families with daughters lived in terrible fear of surprise visits from the Soviet partisans, or other random groups that prowled the increasingly lawless region. They were happy to have the Polish partisans around, and to have an armed soldier in the home was a blessing to them, short as his stay was. When he departed and said his goodbyes, the family invited him back for a visit after the war, in more peaceful circumstances. It was a pleasant thought.

During his recuperation, he had plenty of time to think. He had already witnessed so much death and violence, the awful scenes replaying in waking moments and in dreams. He had killed other men. He was getting hardened to it all and wondered if he would suffer some permanent and damaging changes to his personality and character. *Would he become a remorseless killer?*

Józef again thought about the mentality of the Germans and Russians, and how they degenerated quickly into such savage behavior. In a new world free of restrictions and restraint, man's worst impulses seemed to take over. In his meetings with the Russian partisans, Józef had no doubt that in a different time they could all have been friends. But he felt that the terrible and hopeless ideology that they were brainwashed with left them damaged. The State was their God, and the State did not care about human life, dignity, or mercy. Everything with the communists was a lie. Actions that lead to abuse and murder had to be justified always as good and helpful and just.

The Germans were even more brutal, but almost opposite in mentality. No denials or pretending about their motives and methods was needed. They seemed proud of the cruelty and ruthlessness. They documented it.

So far, his fellow Polish soldiers had held on to humanity in the face of extreme duress. They were fighting in their own homeland for their own people. They had strict orders against abusing any local inhabitants of any ethnic group. But mostly it seemed to be their deep Christian culture and upbringing that provided the guardrails. Józef knew he was not as pious and faithful as many of the men, but he felt God's presence in his life and hoped that the culture of his upbringing would carry him through without losing his soul. There would be a lot more killing to do, unfortunately, before the end of this war.

During the last week of October, Józef was back with the partisans but on light duty. The doctor told him to start playing his accordion if possible, as the best way to get back some dexterity. It was a terrible process at first, painful and stiff fingers could barely make anything sound like music. But slow progress was made. He felt better and better about the future use of his hand as the weeks went on.

While on light duty, Józef went into the woods often and practiced with his pistol. He pictured the eventual day when his revenge vow would be satisfied and he would assassinate the murderer Czech from Iwieniec. He imagined sneaking up with the pistol, confronting the monster, and dispatching him coldly. Carefully he closed one eye, lined up the sights, and squeezed out rounds at a wooden plank about twenty feet away.

"That's not how I was trained," came a voice from behind, startling Józef. It was Pilch. *How did he sneak up on me?* thought Józef, the ever-vigilant partisan. "What do you mean?" he asked.

"In special operations training, we discussed the different uses for different weapons. For accuracy and aiming with sights, we discounted pistols as inferior. They trained us to use pistols for short range and quick action, and we learned to aim by 'feel' rather than the slow process you are doing."

Pilch put out his hand and Józef handed him the pistol. Pilch then held the pistol out in front of his chest area rather casually, then suddenly fired twice. Both shots hit the target just inches apart. Józef was impressed.

"How do you learn that?" Józef asked.

"Only with repetition," Pilch answered. "But some could never get good at it, which would be a very key thing to know ahead of time, before you get into a bad situation."

Pilch then patted him on the shoulder and walked off, silently. Józef tried a few shots without the sights, missing completely. For the partisans, always desperate to keep their ammunition supply stocked, each bullet was precious. He couldn't afford not to learn from each mistake. Józef walked to the target and searched the area behind the plank to find out where the misses went and recalculate. He returned to practice as often as possible, and made some small gains in accuracy and speed. Again, Józef pictured the confrontation with Czech. Perhaps there would be bodyguards to take out also? *This skill could be a life saver,* he thought.

Chapter Fourteen

THE SAVING OF WALMA

THAT AUTUMN, WORD CAME in from the partisan informant network that the Germans were planning a punitive expedition to the small and nearby town of Walma. Pilch immediately formed a plan to save the little town from possible annihilation. Józef and his cavalry were sent over with plans for a defensive stand. They were two days early so they camped nearby at the outskirts of the town, so as to not alert anyone.

Józef rode back to see Pilch for meetings and a final planning session. The relaxed discussion soon ended with a shock. A courier burst into the headquarters with a panicked demeanor and interrupted.

"Something went wrong with our information, or the Germans changed plans. They have launched their operation and are right now driving fast to Walma."

Józef jumped up and ran out the door. He did not need anyone to explain that not only was the town in grave danger, but his unaware soldiers could be caught by surprise and wiped out. He ran to his horse, which was tied up in a line with some others, one of which was Jan's Bucephalus. The horse had been bouncing around between soldiers but hadn't found a permanent master. A sudden intuition overtook him, and Józef untied Jan's old horse instead of his own, and jumped on.

Józef instantly felt a power he had never experienced before as he spurred Bucephalus and charged him forward with kicks and shouts. In seconds they were galloping at top speed and Józef crouched down and hung on tightly for the first kilometer. The consistent speed was amazing and scary. It felt like they were flying, with the powerful horse's hooves just rhythmically thumping the ground at great intervals, as if to only remind them of a tenuous connection to the earth.

Up ahead Józef spotted a dust cloud moving along a distant road to the right. *It's them,* he realized, *we have to beat them to the crossroads or all will be lost.* Józef needed to continue on this road to his base camp while the enemy stayed on the main road to the town. If they got there first he would be effectively blocked, and he would probably get shot. If he waited for them to pass he would be way too late to save anyone. Bucephalus saw the column too and slightly slowed.

"Go, go, go!" Józef yelled, spurring him on. Amazingly, the horse found another level of speed and ran harder, as if understanding the dire situation. Perhaps no one after Jan had let the horse use his true gift and just run free with total abandon. The road curved toward the oncoming column and passed along a wood fence. Bucephalus leaned into the curve and hugged the fence line so tight that Józef had the terrifying fear that every new post would tear his leg off at the knee, but each one flashed by, missed by mere inches.

They approached the crossroads and it was going to be close. Józef had lost his cap, and with difficulty began unbuttoning his uniform shirt while hanging on with the other hand. The shirt slipped off one side and flapped behind him until he shook it off his right wrist and it fluttered away and down to the ground far behind him. Now, he hoped, he looked like a farm hand and not a partisan, as he rode on bare chested.

The Germans were going to spot him for sure. Józef could clearly see the trucks and armored cars racing along as the two roads angled toward the crossing. He and Bucephalus hit the crossroads just yards ahead of the first German truck. As he flashed by, he saw some Germans stand up and point at him, but he flew past and was leaving the intersection behind before they could even raise a rifle. He pushed the sweaty and foaming horse for several more minutes until arriving at the camp. He jumped off, feeling wobbly in the legs from the excitement and strain of the ride, and yelled out to his men, "The enemy is arriving in mere minutes!"

They jumped to attention and started grabbing their weapons. The original plan was defunct as they would not have time to set up. They would attack the arriving Germans instead, and hope for the best.

The Nazi SS unit roared into the town and vehicle after vehicle screeched to a stop. Soldiers jumped down and immediately started entering the first few houses, sending the terrified occupants out into the streets with shouting and violent shoves. They were methodically moving along, but when they approached the fourth and fifth houses, shots suddenly rang out and some German soldiers fell down dead. The partisans had just arrived, running into the line of houses from behind and to the right side. The surprised SS men turned their forces toward the threat, only to have the second wave of partisans open fire from the left. Józef had split them into two groups, so as to attack from both sides.

A fierce battle commenced with soldiers from both armies firing at any available target. The Poles, attacking from between the houses, had better cover than the enemy, who had mostly been caught in the middle of the street. A German officer ran out briefly to direct his men, was hit in the lower body and fell to his knees. A second later a shot to the head dropped him permanently. Some of the German soldiers were using their vehicles as protection. That's when the grenades began to fly, and trucks exploded into flames. This sent soldiers running away, with many soon falling in the Polish crossfire.

The battle slowed down to a cat and mouse game of soldiers running into each other between houses and other hiding places, with mini-gun battles exploding at each encounter. But this phase also turned to the Poles' favor, as the townspeople began pointing out the location of the enemies that they could easily spot from the upper windows of their houses.

When every German vehicle was disabled and most of their men killed, the last few surrendered by walking out into the open with arms raised.

More Polish cavalry arrived, having been sent by Pilch. They missed the battle but partook in a celebration as the village set up tables of food and drink for their rescuers. Some of the old *Babcias* could not stop crying and hugging the soldiers, as they relived the fear and the thought of what could have been.

Józef later walked over and checked on Bucephalus. A local farm boy was brushing him down, as per Józef's request.

"You saved a town," Józef said to the animal while patting its neck. Despite being tired and sweaty, the horse looked entirely pleased with itself, bobbing its head and snorting. Later, because none of the soldiers wanted to try and make Bucephalus their regular horse - he was just too willful and resistant to direction - Józef was allowed to give the horse away to the thrilled farm boy.

"Every once in a while, take him for a real hard run," Józef told the boy.

Chapter Fifteen

THE DELUGE

THE SOVIET LEADERS Dubov and Wasilewsky visited the Polish camp in October and asked permission to speak to the men. Pilch mulled it over for a moment and then granted permission. He knew his men and knew the Soviets, so Pilch decided this act of politeness would do no harm. He walked out with the Soviet officers and asked the men to gather up and give their "friends" the courtesy of some attention.

Dubov then stood on a wagon and began a speech full of Soviet slogans and propaganda. Pilch sat off to the side. His soldiers could see from his subtle facial expressions that he wasn't taking the speech seriously at all. The diatribe about the glories of communism went on and on and on. Soldiers in the back were the first to slink away. As the speech dragged on, more and more Poles drifted off, until at the conclusion, there were only a dozen or so left listening. Dubov wrapped things up, thanked Pilch, and then he and Wasilewsky rode off abruptly.

In early November some new officers were sent in from regional command to aid the fast-growing partisan army. Major Wacław Pełka was placed in charge and Pilch was appointed second in leadership. Along with Pełka came two additional officers and an officer-cadet.

Pilch, Miłaszewski, and Nurkiewicz became privately concerned that Pełka was too trusting of the Soviets in the area. He seemed to give them the benefit of the doubt, which the local men had long since abandoned. Orders were very clear from Warsaw leadership that good relations with the Russians were to be pursued to fight the common enemy. Experience had painfully taught the local commanders that this was a goal largely based in hope and not reality.

Even now, Russian units kept dropping by unannounced for suspicious visits. They were obviously scouting out the Polish forces. Some Polish partisans were suspected as spies and were watched carefully.

An incident occurred when Nurkiewicz caught a Russian partisan group ransacking a Polish village at gunpoint. They were supposedly members of Zorin's group, which had a terrible reputation and had been warned before. Nurkiewicz's men were accused of shooting five of the bandits.

Soviet envoys showed up at the Polish headquarters and demanded Nurkiewicz be handed over for judgment. The Poles refused to give up their cavalry commander, but the Russians returned days later, again demanding Nurkiewicz to be tried by Soviet authorities. Shockingly, Major Pełka seemed open to this and was leaning towards appeasing the communists. Pilch and Miłaszewski intervened respectfully and suggested a joint investigation before any final decisions were made. A trip to the scene was unable to locate any bodies or proof of any kind, so the controversy died down and Nurkiewicz stayed safe. The whole incident was alarming. The local Poles were left wondering how one of their own leaders could be so accommodating to an adversary?

On November 11, Poland's Independence Day, the partisans held an outdoor Mass and ceremonial parade in the town of Derewno. Large flocks of local townspeople joined in, making it a huge event. Hearts were filled with patriotism and pride.

Aleksander Warakomski returned to give a rousing speech about Poland's indivisibility and refusal to accede to territorial losses. Addressing the crowds, he assured them that Poland would fight to restore their freedom and independence.

The events were of course noticed by the Soviets, much to their anger. They began a strong propaganda assault in published papers, referring to the Poles as "fascists and reactionaries." But propaganda would prove to be the least of the danger, as devious schemes were already being ordered and put into motion. The betrayal of Poles had already occurred in other nearby regions, leading to the capture and subsequent murder of entire Polish units. The same trap was being set up again, and the Stołpce-Naliboki group were the next designated victims.

On November 27, General Dubov of the Soviet Brigades of the Iwieniec region sent an invitation to Pełka and several other Polish officers to meet for a war council to discuss combined operations against the Germans. The proposed meeting was set up for December 1, 1943 at 7 am. Officers Miłaszewski, Los, and Parchimowicz were also asked to attend, but had strong reservations. They were overruled by Pełka's wishes. All in all, ten officers of the Polish command agreed to go to the meeting. Nurkiewicz was a blunt and clear-thinking man and his strong admonitions against this meeting bordered on insolence toward Pełka. He asked to take his cavalry on various missions elsewhere, and was allowed to do just that.

On that frosty early morning at six o'clock, the officers left camp and rode down the trail to the meeting with a small escort of soldiers. After traveling a short distance down the trail they were ambushed by Soviet troops and disarmed quickly. The captured Poles were marched off to the Soviet camp some kilometers away, except Miłaszewski. He was escorted back at gunpoint and ordered to assemble his men for surrender. The Polish camp was, by then, being surrounded by over a thousand armed Soviet soldiers.

Adolf Pilch had just finished breakfast when the disarmed Miłaszewski was returned under guard. The Russians were telling Miłaszewski to order his men to hand over their weapons.

Pilch immediately recognized the threat and escaped from the trap. He ran down a trail through the woods to warn the other nearby Polish camp. Upon arrival, he quickly explained the situation, and asked the men whether they preferred to make an escape or to attempt a rescue. In one voice, all wanted to fight for their comrades. They headed out just as more Russian troops were moving in as part of the same coordinated attack.

As they approached the first camp, they saw all the disarmed Polish partisans lined up in rows guarded by machine guns. The Russians spotted the rescuers and called out to them that any attack would have them open fire on the captured men. There could be no rescue. The Polish camp was being wildly looted by the undisciplined Russian soldiers. Everything was being taken.

Pilch and his men had to get away from the swarming Soviets, but found the roads and paths all guarded. The only escape was into the boggy forest area that bordered one side of the camp. It took seven exhausting and grueling hours to make their way out of the entrapment zone. With each step the ice would briefly hold before breaking, and then their feet would sink so deep that the freezing mud would reach above the knees. Exhausted and nearly frozen to death, the stragglers finally came upon some miserable huts where burned-out survivors of *Operation Hermann* had taken up residence. The poor but generous folk warmed them up and shared their modest food.

The following day, Pilch and his dozen men arrived in the small town of Brodek. There they began to understand the full scope of the disaster. They learned that the first company had also been attacked in Derewno by Soviet brigades. Men who fought back were lined up and shot. Wounded men were tortured and then killed. Two brothers had refused to give up and kept brawling until thoroughly overcome, and then were hideously abused. They were found dead but not before they had their fingers and ears cut off. A Russian man named Frolow, who stayed with the Poles after marrying a Polish girl, was found hanged. The bulk of the captured men had been marched off to the Soviet camps. Only the cavalry had completely avoided capture.

Commander Nurkiewicz had been on patrol and received word of gunfire being heard in Derewno, so dispatched a unit to investigate. The group stumbled upon large Russian forces and were disarmed, but the patrol leader Jan Jakubowski charged away and escaped. When Nurkiewicz arrived with a larger force he found two dead Polish partisans in the town square, but the Russians were gone. They searched the town and found a few more bodies of Polish soldiers. Nurkiewicz's men later captured a large group of Soviet partisans, but with no home base and no plan on what to do next, they released them all.

Józef was on patrol when he first discovered some escaped Polish partisans and heard the shocking news of the attacks. He linked up with Nurkiewicz and they used their combined cavalry to search for more stragglers. Quite a few men had used their first chance to slip away and rejoin the Polish Army.

The Polish officers captured in the morning were offered the opportunity to abandon the Polish Home army and join the Soviet forces. They strongly refused, so five of them were immediately sentenced to death and shot. Five others were taken away by plane to Moscow for show trials and then to the Lubyanka prison, including Miłaszewski and Pełka.

The Polish regular soldiers were to be absorbed into Red partisan units, but this Soviet plan was a total failure. The patriotic men were impervious to the constant communist attempts at brainwashing and always looked for escape. Once this was realized, the Russians began shooting Polish soldiers in the back while marching through the forest. All through the following spring the melting snow gradually revealed frozen corpses to the families searching desperately for their loved ones.

On December 3rd, the cavalry received an alert from scouts that a group of men were approaching. It turned out to be Pilch and about 30 other survivors. Their half dead physical appearance was shocking. They hadn't slept since the attack and had had very little food. They were encrusted with dried mud and their clothes were in tatters. Pilch had bloodshot eyes and was pale from his ordeal. Together, the reunited men assessed their bleak situation. They had altogether fewer than fifty men left, and had lost their camps, their supplies, and most of their weapons to the Soviets. They were on the run and being pursued by large numbers of Russian partisans, in addition to the ever present Nazis. No town was safe to even enter without fear of Russian or German surveillance.

The group first attempted to take shelter in the village of Ossow but was immediately attacked by Russian partisans and had to flee.

Another level of misery and desperation then entered the picture. Word came that many of their local families were being targeted by the Soviets with threats and violence. Individuals were beaten, including an eighty-two year old father of one of the men. Some family members were murdered as threats were made for the not-yet-captured Poles to give up and surrender to Soviet authorities.

The small troop fought several more skirmishes to escape attacks and was almost out of ammunition. After days on the run with no sleep or food, under constant attack, the Poles were near the end of all hope. For some, it was too much to bear. Sixteen members of the cavalry abandoned their duties and disappeared. The deluge had come.

It was at this time that an envoy reached them with a message from the local German command in Iwieniec. The Germans were aware of the Russian attacks and wanted to negotiate an agreement. What they first proposed was a joint fight against the Russians, but the Poles would never be allies in this manner with the hated occupiers. Pilch discussed it with the men, wanting to hear all opinions. They were, by then, in open warfare against the Russians. If they could only rearm, they would have a chance. A chance to survive. A chance to fight back. A chance to save their families. Annihilation was coming otherwise.

Everyone was for a modified deal: a temporary ceasefire with the Germans in exchange for weapons. Pilch realized that if the German authorities actually knew how small the remaining number of Polish partisans was, and how desperate their situation was, that a deal would never have been struck. He bluffed, implying that there were still hundreds of men in the field, not the few dozen in reality.

The Germans were actually eager to have a reprieve from Polish ambushes. The Eastern Front situation was degenerating for them, and they needed every break they could get. Pilch negotiated the deal. A ceasefire with the local German occupation was agreed to, in exchange for help obtaining weapons. The Germans then gave Pilch locations to easily sweep in and pick up guns and ammunition.

Even though it was a life-and-death decision for the soldiers and their local families, the ceasefire was an agonizing choice. None of them ever wanted to be judged as friendly to the enemy. But their primary duty was to stay alive so they could continue to fight Poland's enemies. *Let us have the guns and ammunition, then we decide who and when to fight.* It was understood that without the weapons, there could be no future.

Pilch wrote out a report of the situation and sent it on to regional headquarters. Because it was a local agreement, it did not save Aleksander Warakomski from being caught and murdered by the Gestapo on a trip to Lida in January of 1944.

Once rearmed, the Poles began successfully fighting off Soviet attacks. More escapees from the Russian camps kept returning and the Poles began to increase their numbers. After several successful skirmishes with heavy Russian losses, the Poles sent out warnings that any further attacks on civilian family members would bring about devastation for those responsible. The Russians backed off this practice, but continued attacking the partisans. Józef gathered up escaped men, staying vigilant against ambushes.

Pilch reached out to the sixteen men who had deserted. He offered them a chance to return immediately, and with good behavior they would be forgiven. He warned that their refusal, however, meant they would be tried for desertion, which carried a death sentence. Twelve came back and were added back to the fold.

Chapter Sixteen

THE SECRET ORDER

SOME DAYS LATER JÓZEF and his patrol passed through a small village at night and his scouts caught sight of a Russian troop approaching. Józef set up the ambush. First he had men set up hidden sniper positions along the road between the houses. Then the remaining mounted men pulled back.

When the Soviets wandered in, the snipers announced their presence and called for them to halt. Immediately the mounted cavalry showed up both front and rear to block escape. The Russians were outnumbered and surrounded, so made a prudent decision and surrendered. After being disarmed, they were lined up and searched. On the Commissar, Józef made a shocking find.

Neatly folded in a breast pocket was a top secret order from Soviet authorities detailing the plans for the December 1st attack on the Polish partisans. In great detail it listed how, when, where, and by whom the treacherous action would take place. It was definitive proof that this was not some isolated local event, but a purposeful policy right from the top, all the way to Beria and Stalin himself.

Józef decided to release the disarmed Russian patrol. He was a fighter, not an executioner, he reasoned. Later it was learned that the Commissar was shot by his own Soviet comrades for allowing the capture of the secret order. The NKVD also shot the guilty man's common law wife for good measure.

Józef brought the document to Nurkiewicz. Pilch then sent it on to regional command. By courier it made its way all the way to Warsaw's Home Army leaders. General Bor Komorowski attached a note and sent it on to London.

By all accounts the document should have prompted explosive changes to Polish policies as the true diabolical nature of Soviet goals was exposed. But it didn't. It was discounted in seriousness and suspected of being a forgery or misunderstanding. Perhaps it was an example of cognitive dissonance, as the authorities could not grasp the terrible truth of the future ahead. Perhaps good people cannot sometimes believe the evil others are capable of.

The document was largely set aside and policies unchanged. Many years later, after the war, it resurfaced as real proof of Soviet perfidy. In 1952 it was entered into the record at United States congressional hearings, along with the name of the man who captured it, Józef Niedźwiecki.

The translated order follows on the next page.

What happened next in the wild and chaotic eastern borderlands was a war within a war. For the first half of 1944, the Polish and Russian partisans engaged in battle after battle with each other. The Polish group regained strength quickly with the help of many new recruits rushing to join, and with the continued inflow of escapees from the Soviet camps.

Meanwhile, orders still came over radio from Warsaw for the Polish Home Army to report to local Russian units and coordinate actions against the Germans. Pilch, of course, had little choice but to act independently and ignore such directives.

Copy no. 7
Strictly secret (classified)
Battle Order

To: Commanding Officers and Commissars Partisan Stalin Brigade,

30 November, 1943. 1500 hr.

To carry out an order of the chief of staff of the partisan formations at the supreme headquarters of the Red Army, Gen. Lt. Ponomarenko and the authorized main headquarters of the partisan at the headquarters of the chief of staff as ruled by C.P (6) W.B. Baranovitz District, Mat. Gen. Platanov.

On the first day of December, 1943. At exactly 7a.m., in all areas and inhabited parts of the district begin to disarm all members and groups of the Polish (partisan) legion.

All taken arms and printed evidence to be recorded. Disarmed members and groups to be taken to the Polish camp named Miłaszewski in the vicinity of Nesterowich village.

Should there be any resistance on the part of Polish partisans they must be shot on the spot.

From the moment of receiving this order it should be immediately dispatched, in strictly classified letters, to the operating areas of your Groups, Companies, and Platoons, for the execution of this order.

REPEAT: Order to be kept in strict secrecy. The leaders and commanding officers will be responsible for keeping this secret.

COMMANDER "STALIN" BRIGADE Col. Gulewicz
COMMISSAR "STALIN" BRIGADE Lt. Col. Muranov
CHIEF OF STAFF "STALIN" BRIGADE Lt. Col. Karpov

Typed 10 copies:

No. 1 For the Records
No. 2 and 3 Group "Bolshevik"
No. 4 and 5 [Group] "Suvorov"
No. 6 [Group] "Tshapayev"
No. 8 [Group] "Budienny"
No. 9 [Group] "Ryzak"
No. 10 [Group] "October Revolution"
Round Seal - Brigade "Stalin"

Figure 1. Church of Saint Michael the Archangel, Iwieniec, Poland (today Belarus).

Figure 2. The Amazon Women: Lancer Helena Niedźwiecka, centered between Medics Jadwiga Bałabuszko and Alina Pietrucka.

Figure 3. Commanders of AK Stołpecki Group. Major Pilch is third from the left, Józef is fifth from the left. Fr. Hilary Praczyński is in the long coat, between the children.

Figure 4. Józef Niedźwiecki with Jan Niedźwiecki.

Figure 5. Lieutenant Józef Niedźwiecki with Virtuti Militari.

Figure 6. Kostuchy, May 1944.

Figure 7. Mass in Derewno.

Figure 8. Mass in Derewno.

Figure 9 Adolf Pilch on the march, September 1944. Jan Jakubowski is first from the right, and Pilch is second from the right

Figure 10. Mass in Kampinos Forest.

Figure 11. Józef with Adolf Pilch.

Figure 12. Corporal Kazimierz Jankowski, Rome, 1946

Figure 13. In England.

Figure 14. Józef playing the accordian

Figure 15. Józef and Helena in England.

Figure 16. Casarano, Italy. January 24, 1946

Figure 17. Helena Niedzwiecka

Figure 18. Helena with Franciszek Rybka.

Figure 19. Captain Franciszek Rybka.

Figure 20. Helena in nursing school in England.

Figure 21. From left to right: Adolf Pilch, Pilch's wife Eva, Helena and Józef.

Figure 22. Józef's wife Paulina.

Figure 23. Partisans Frank Kosowicz and Kazimierz Jankowski at Józef and Paulina's wedding.

Figure 24. General Bór-Komorowski visting Buffalo, fourth from the left. Józef is in the back row.

Figure 25. Zygmunt Otto Roman Lakocinski, a Polish professor from Sweden, who interviewed Ravensbruck survivors. Helena was one of the camp survivors interviewed. Pictured here with Józef in England.

Figure 26. The house Józef built with his own hands.

Figure 27. The Forest Soldier at peace.

Chapter Seventeen

SKI ADVENTURE

IN THE DEEP SNOWS of midwinter the volume of fighting slowed, with the exception of a few chance encounters and a few planned actions.

Pilch approached Sergeant *Gray* with one such plan. A Red partisan unit had taken over several houses in a small hamlet and turned out the residents. The owners had complained to the Home Army, reporting that the Russians previously had some of the captured Polish soldiers still under their command. Some of the Poles had run off and were unaccounted for, but others had been killed before getting away.

"There is an opportunity here," said Pilch, "to rescue our men and destroy this unit, and return the homes to our citizens. It's totally snowed in by this storm and isolated, it will be a complete surprise."

Pilch went through the details of his plan and offered Józef time to consider. But Józef answered right away.

"Sounds good, I will pick out some men."

Six of them loaded their gear into the truck and drove many difficult miles to the demarcation point, getting stuck several times in the drifting snow. They jumped out at the base of a logging trail, dressed in the winter white hooded overcoats and pants. Each carried their weapons and a backpack of survival gear.

They unloaded cross country skis, fastened them to their boots, and glided off down the trail as the driver turned around and headed back. The snow was deep in the woods in these higher elevations and would have been impassable on foot, but the skis displaced their weight and allowed steady progress. For four hours, they traversed the silent woodlands as snow continued to fall. The birches and spruce along the wide paths arched inward under the snows and created the feeling of a long cathedral hall, with the white-clad soldiers processing along below in single file like pilgrims.

As dusk approached they reached the last leg of the journey and looked for a suitable camping spot. The temperature was dropping with the sunset and the plan was to eat, get a few hours sleep, and then proceed to the target before dawn. The men, all chosen for their winter survival experience with the scouts, pulled out their folding shovels and began digging two caves into a huge snowdrift. It was after dark when they made themselves comfortable on tarpaulins inside the igloo-like enclosures, three men per cave. Their body heat and a single candle created a warm enough environment that after eating the men fell asleep quickly.

Józef was not ready or able to sleep, so he listened to the gusting wind outside and ran through the next day's plan in his mind. Some time later the wolves started howling. He had heard them many times in his life, but the distinctive cry always brought forth deep feelings. It was a truly wild and beautiful sound. Although wolves posed little real risk, the howls and yips still struck a small chord of innate fear. It was a deep-seated human reaction to a wild predator. Józef continued to listen and then said to himself, *we are not so different, you and us, sometimes hunted, sometimes the hunters.*

He may have dozed off for a little while but was alert and ready at three in the morning.

"Get up men, let's go," he called out.

They all did a weapons check, then headed out into a bright moonlit night. The snow had stopped and everything was calm and glistening. The night was so bright that one could see everything clearly. They pushed their way up the last hill for an hour and then looked down at the cluster of homes below. It was a peaceful and beautiful scene, as the homes were nestled in a little valley with open farm fields around them and small barns near each home. Józef sent the best skier down first and then they all followed his perfect tracks. It was a long and smooth run down the open hillside, and once they started they glided silently and easily until the ground flattened out near the first cottage.

They unfastened their skis and then moved forward on foot, sneaking up to the first house. Józef crept along the wall until he was under the window, then crouched and listened for several minutes. Very slowly, he rose up until he could just barely peer over the windowsill. His eyes adjusted to the dim light of the interior, as a few embers in the fireplace cast a glow on the room. The shapes of sleeping men were faintly visible, and Józef noted their number and location.

A Russian soldier sat at the table but appeared asleep with chin on chest. Was he supposed to be guarding? A bottle and glass sat on the table in front of him. They moved off to the next home and then the next, scouting out the number of men in each room. Everyone was asleep. Weapons were mostly aligned neatly in one corner, but some had arms nearby.

"Check the barns quickly and come right back," Józef whispered to one of his men.

"There are no enemies in the barns," reported his man after returning. "There is a Polish soldier hanging from a rafter."

Józef clenched his jaw at this, then gave out instructions, and two men headed to each house. In a few seconds they were all in place. Józef walked right in through the front door.

It was over quickly. At each location the two men walked in and yelled "Hands up! Surrender!" Immediately several of the Russians reached for their weapons and were gunned down. The rest were quickly hustled outside and lined up to stand in the cold and snow. One of the leaders questioned what was to be their fate. Józef explained that they would have a quick military trial witnessed by the locals, and that they would likely be executed for murdering Polish partisans.

The Russian nodded and asked if they could put on their boots, since they were standing in the snow. Józef let them go in one at a time under guard. The others were whispering amongst themselves. When the last man came out the prisoners all bolted, running away toward the nearest woods. Józef's men raised their machine guns, but Józef called off the shooting. It felt unseemly to shoot unarmed men in the back. The coatless and hatless men had little chance of survival in the frigid temperatures anyway.

The team then opened the doors and windows of the cottages to let out the smoke from the gunfire, and began dragging the bodies out and laying them in the snow. They planned to stay in the homes for at least a few days. They would contact the locals and search for their Polish soldiers.

The next day one of the families arrived by horse and sledge. They had already spotted the change in occupants. After thanking the Polish troops profusely, they told the story of the days before the Home Army group arrival. First the Reds came in and stayed with them, demanding food and shelter. Several Polish soldiers had run off in the snow storm and the Russians killed the few that didn't get away. They chased some runners down and shot them in the woods, then hung a captured man. Afterwards the Russians decided to stay longer and more comfortably, so they threw the families right out into the cold. This family had fled to the home of relatives some distance away. It was clear the family hated the Russian partisans with burning contempt and Józef wondered what other abuse they had suffered in addition to theft of their homes and the observed murders.

The family immediately went to work reclaiming the property. The father and son started loading the dead bodies into the sledge. They would take them deep into the forest, lest any future Soviet troops find out what happened. Two older women began cleaning the blood from the floors. Later they prepared some food for everyone, all the while remaining very stoic and serious.

The family was amazed that just six men had wiped out the Russian unit, and asked how this was possible. One of Józef's soldiers volunteered, "When leader *Gray* attacks, he hits the enemy like an avalanche!" bringing laughter from his men.

At dinner that night toasts were made. The family and his soldiers were feeling celebratory, and Józef did his best to go along. It would be a welcome distraction from thinking about the killing.

"To my wolf pack" Józef called out and threw back his glass with everyone. *"Sto lat."* The hosts poured out another.

"To Sergeant *Avalanche!*" someone shouted out, eliciting loud cheers and another drink.

The other families returned the next day, along with the several Polish partisans who had escaped. They had also hid out with locals, but were expecting a Russian search party to hunt for them when the weather broke. Józef's crew stayed on comfortably for a few days until the snowing stopped, then headed back to the partisan camp with all their men.

Chapter Eighteen

FIGHTING THE SOVIETS

WHEN SPRING THAWS MELTED the ice and snow the frequency of fighting between Soviet and Polish partisans resumed. The Russians continued searching for any and all opportunities to attack. They often anticipated Polish movements through their network of spies, so the Poles began a practice of always changing plans at the last minute to avoid ambushes. In March, the Polish cavalry was attacked several times while on patrol, losing some men but inflicting losses in return. In mid-May, the Russians launched a major attack against Poles staying in the town of Kamien. The night raid turned into a deadly battle with twenty-one Poles killed and over eighty lost to the attackers. Longin Kołosowski was a hero of the battle, despite suffering serious injuries.

As the spring fighting continued into Summer, over 100 skirmishes or full battles took place. The Soviets suffered large numbers of dead and wounded.

On one occasion, the communists decided to attack the Poles as they attended Mass, hoping to trap them unawares for a quick slaughter. As the hundreds of Soviet soldiers surrounded the little wooden church, they were spotted by well-placed lookouts who sounded the alarm. The Poles were able to exit the church quickly and fight their way out of the trap with few casualties.

It was in June that the chance meeting with Czech finally occurred. Józef was on a quick mission along the outskirts of Iwieniec with three of his men. They were in the German zone of control, so they were safe during the ceasefire, but carried their arms. They rounded a corner and across the street saw a group of six or seven German soldiers.

Józef suddenly spotted Czech in the back of the group chatting with his huge bodyguard. In an instant, Józef lost his composure as seething hatred took over. He pulled up his short machine gun, yelling at the soldiers to get out of the way as he ran towards them.

"I just want Sawinola!" he shouted. Czech turned white and looked at the crazed Pole as all his men snapped up their weapons. Czech drew his pistol and aimed back, but his hand was shaking with fear. The bodyguard moved in front of Czech and everyone was yelling now. Józef tried moving to the left for a clear shot but became aware of his own men yelling in his ear, "Don't do it! This is crazy!"

The Germans had all their guns trained on the Polish group, but also held fire. Their sergeant then spoke rather calmly to Józef in decent Polish, "Do you want to cancel the ceasefire? You four can be the first to die."

Józef came to his senses, and lowered his weapon. He immediately turned away and walked off, his head pounding, and his men were relieved to follow and get away. When they were out of range Józef's emotions bubbled up and he let out a deep guttural shout of pure frustration. His men just looked at him, surprised by their typically composed leader.

When more time had passed by, Józef thought about how foolhardy his actions were. He had nearly put his own personal vow of revenge over everyone else, and it could have had disastrous results. He made a new vow to purge as much selfishness and emotion from his leadership as possible.

It was a shocking incident for the Germans, and a short time later Sawinola was transferred out of Iwieniec and disappeared, presumably for his own safety. Whatever happened to him is largely a mystery with several conflicting accounts. Some say he was caught years later by Polish authorities and punished for his crimes. Others say he was never found again. One account says that Józef Niedźwiecki had another opportunity, and killed Czech in a secret manner, but there is no definitive proof to state any ending with certainty.

Even though the Poles were losing some men in these battles with the Soviets, their overall numbers continued to grow. They increased to over eight hundred men and women soldiers with the continued influx of new volunteers that poured in from every village around the region.

Adolf Pilch created a new atmosphere of leadership. He always wanted to know what his officers' opinions were on different actions and how best to handle challenges. After listening carefully, he provided his final decisions and orders. The strict demarcation between ranks softened. Closeness and mutual respect grew in the ranks as the men realized that their field experience and thinking were highly valued. Pilch always gave his officers the freedom to make the instant decisions necessary when on their own in the field, and his trust and high expectations made the soldiers infinitely stronger and more effective. There continued to be an emphasis on keeping the soldiers alive. Unnecessary risks were avoided and careful planning was the norm.

During the course of early 1944, the group was largely left alone without help or direction from regional or Warsaw command. The Russian front was advancing, the Germans were retreating, and the east was in a chaotic mess. The burning question was where would this, by then substantial, partisan army go next?

It seemed that a plan was being formed to attack and retake the city of Wilno. This was far to the north through dangerous occupied territory, but word came that the Stołpce-Naliboki group may be sent to aid this endeavor. Pilch sent his deputy commander and fellow Cichociemni Franciszek Rybka on a fact finding mission north to clarify. Rybka reported back that this task was impossible. One could never move an army through this territory full of German troops and the approaching Red Army. They didn't even have a proposed route or any maps.

Pilch brought fifteen of his officers together for discussions on these proposed plans to head north. It seemed like pure folly to the men, but they waited for orders. Major Kalenkiewicz of the Nowogródek region sent word that he would send plans and help for this action, as the region then fell under Wilno's command leadership. No plans, help, or maps were ever forthcoming in the rapidly changing situation, and the Stołpce-Naliboki group was left twisting in the wind.

In close proximity and of major concern to the north were also five hundred men from the SS RONA (Russkaya Osvoboditelnaya Narodnaya Armiya) Battalion. This was a group of Russians from the Lokot district of Russia, that in hopes of gaining autonomy from the Soviet Union, had joined the Nazis and formed into a large army. They were also known as the Kaminski Brigade, after their leader Bronislaw Kaminski. They developed a reputation as murderous pillagers, and were specialized in anti-partisan warfare.

The paths of RONA and Pilch's men would soon cover similar journeys, leading to several deadly encounters on the way to Warsaw. The journeys would be similar in geography, but their moral paths were divergent. The communist-raised, but Nazi-by-choice battalion would devolve deeply into debauchery and demonic evil before the fateful final battles in Kampinos forest.

On the 23rd of June, artillery from the Russian front could be heard rumbling in the distance. The Polish partisans knew their fate if caught by the massive Red Army. The Soviets had already arrived at the outskirts of Minsk.

Pilch contacted the partisans in Rakow and also any locally allied Belarussian police to join him immediately to combine forces. Still he waited, but all contacts and orders from command had dried up. In a last-ditch effort, Pilch contacted the leadership in Baranowicze to ask for instructions, and was shocked to find that they had already evacuated and were gone. He moved the army to Slonim and found command there also long gone, although they added twenty additional partisan volunteers there.

There was no longer time for delay and a decision had to be made. They had to leave the region and head west, away from the Russian onslaught. Word of the planned Warsaw Uprising had filtered in and that was something that they could potentially reach and aid. First they would have to make a dangerous six hundred and thirty-nine kilometer trek through occupied territory with a nine hundred person column. Perhaps this partisan army, having already survived incredible odds in both *Operation Hermann* and the Soviet betrayal, could achieve one more miracle.

The operation to take Wilno was a disaster for the Polish side. Those that made it there had little success initially and had to join up with the Russians to dislodge the Germans. But when large numbers of the Red Army arrived the Poles were all disarmed. Many were sent to gulags. The officers were arrested or killed.

Chapter Nineteen

THE TREK - SECOND INJURY

ON JUNE 28TH the Stołpce-Naliboki group slowly began the momentous undertaking of leaving the borderlands. They were joined by many family members that also decided to flee the oncoming Russian front. The large number of civilians and wagons added logistical difficulty, but the problems were worked out and a well-organized effort commenced on the 29th. Initially there was a lot of troop movement and heavy traffic along the route. They spotted shattered German units retreating on the same roads. Some haggard troops were virtually unarmed, and damaged vehicles of all types were left abandoned along roadways. Though the Poles aroused interest and suspicion, these bedraggled German outfits left the partisans alone. The Belarus police at the head of the column confused the situation and the dangerous looking and well-armed Poles dissuaded interest in confrontation.

On the 30th they crossed the Niemen river. It was a clear day so the river looked as blue and reflective as if it were a painting. Józef trotted busily up and down the line and was vaguely aware that everyone's attention was focused on looking at the river. It was only when he reached Helena, and saw her tearful eyes, that he realized the significance of the moment. The river was an important symbol of their home region. They were passing over it and leaving it behind, heading off into a dangerous and unknown fate. He found himself now transfixed in thought as he looked upon the waters. *How many of us will return?* he wondered. *Will I ever see the Niemen again?*

Józef paid attention to the column singing "Za Niemen" once again as they crossed, and heard the stanza that gave him chills:

*My darling, you won't come back.
Your heart will withdraw, your memory will forget.
Look, your horse has already left his pasture and stall,
and on the red battlefield no doubt is your grave."*

The partisans crossed highways and bridges as quickly as possible in the heavy traffic to minimize interactions at choke points. They began traveling country roads at night, then hiding out and resting in forest areas from a few hours after dawn until sunset.

On July 1, 1944 they suffered an attack. They were moving along the edge of the town of Baranowicze on a quiet road with some woodlands to the left. On their right was a low stone wall bordering a small farm field. The column head came under sudden machine gun fire from the forest edge. Two of the cavalry squadrons were thrown momentarily into chaos as horses bucked and bolted and several men were hit.

Józef charged along the column and began rallying the leading squadron into an escape forward, past the firing guns. He then swiveled to turn the oncoming rear column back towards the direction from which they had come. They had to get out of the fire zone quickly and then organize a defense. The split between the groups grew as the back retreated and took cover and the cavalry galloped forward.

Józef turned and raced back to join his escaping squadron and quickly caught up to the last horse and wagon. He recognized that it was his man Kazimierz Jankowski, who was pulling a mounted machine gun behind his horse. It was at this moment that a volley of bullets struck Józef's horse and it leapt wildly, throwing him off onto the ground next to the stone wall. The injured horse continued kicking wildly and then ran off, so Józef quickly vaulted over the stone wall as another volley of bullets clanked off the fieldstones. He was suddenly aware of an intense pain in his lower leg and spotted a round hole in the calf of his tall leather boot. An explosion blew out part of the stone wall several feet away. Józef realized he was the only remaining target left on this stretch of road, as the split Polish column escaped in two directions. He was pinned down and attracting attention from the machine guns and grenades. He had lost his weapon and had no way to escape or fight back. Looking up he was amazed to see Kazimierz turning his horse and cart around and then kicking his horse into a mad dash back to the rescue. Kazimierz had witnessed Józef's fall and without hesitation was riding back fast for his commander.

With bullets whizzing all around, Kazimierz pulled up to Józef and reigned the horse hard. The expression on his face was so remarkably calm and passive despite the hailstorm of bullets, that Józef would never forget the sight of it. Józef immediately clambered back over the wall and jumped into the cart, laying as flat as possible as Kazimierz made another big turn and raced off again. All the while bullets clanked off the machine gun and cart, but somehow never struck the brave man riding the horse.

They reached the rest of the cavalry and Józef limped over to assess the situation. The woodline seemed to come alive as enemy soldiers began advancing out towards the Polish column that had moved to the back. The Poles would have to slow down these German attackers and prevent them from overwhelming the still chaotic retreat of slower infantry and horse-drawn carts. Józef took a step, but tumbled down as his leg gave way. Two men lifted him quickly, alarmed. He felt woozy for a second but recovered and gave out his orders to the squadron. "Arm up and go back along the stone wall. Stay low, crawl if you have to, spread out and open fire as fast as possible."

His experienced partisans moved with efficiency and speed and the first were firing within seconds. Crawling past each other behind the long wall, a shooter would pop up every few yards until a long battle line was formed. Soon the onrushing attackers were getting cut down in numbers. Once suppressing fire was underway, Józef sent cavalry to race farther down the line, where they set up more powerful RKM machine guns. The charge of the enemy was halted, forcing them to retreat back to the woodline and regroup. Józef recognized them as SS RONA men.

The Polish column diverted across the farm field under protection of the cavalry units firing, and a fighting retreat was organized. The dizziness hit back harder, and Józef had to sit down. He pulled his bloody boot off painfully to see the clean entry hole in his calf, which was slowly pulsing blood. He just sat, feeling dazed, and was afraid of passing out. He could see the Polish cavalry being now directed by first squadron leader Jan Jakubowski. They were in good positions already when he saw Pilch arrive. Three of his men returned. "We're getting you out of here" they said.

Two Poles were killed in the attack and thirteen injured. The partisans were able to retreat out of danger, and the RONA forces, having lost more men than the Poles and seeing the organized defense formed, called off their ambush near nightfall and withdrew.

Józef's fast actions were credited with staving off a potential disaster. The 1st and 2nd squadrons had fought off a much larger force and kept the column from being surrounded. He was treated in the field, but the surgery to remove the bullet was done on the medical unit wagon. Helena stayed with him.

The following day the doctors gave the shocking news that the wound was infected and the leg would need to be amputated. Józef was adamant to not allow this and in his feverish and weakened state begged Helena to save his leg if he became unconscious. She guarded him, arguing with the doctors for more time to treat the infection. When the Polish column was leaving, Helena arranged for him to ride as comfortably as possible on a hay bed in a wagon. Józef drifted in and out of consciousness for a day while Helena and the Partisans' doctor cleaned and redressed his wound frequently. The infected calf swelled up to gigantic size and the pain was constant and intense. Every bump of the wagon sent a fiery dagger through his body. Helena gently held his leg up for hours at a time to give him a little relief from the shocks. In lucid moments Józef asked her, "Are you ok? Don't strain yourself." But she always responded with "I am fine," despite her aching arms and back.

Finally, the infection eased and his fever died down. There were discussions about leaving him with a civilian household to recover in better conditions, but he did not want to be left behind. So he continued on with the troop, keeping tabs on his squadron, but riding in the wagon like one of the many family members making the journey.

Chapter Twenty

Journey to Warsaw

With forward scouting the group avoided any large concentrations of German soldiers. On the 15th of July, they crossed the Bug river through a shallow area, carrying equipment above their heads and slowly pulling the wagons through.

On the 16th, Pilch announced that by his order the ceasefire with the Germans was officially over and canceled. The partisans were exuberant and held a Mass to celebrate. Józef reassumed command of his cavalry squadron at this time. He could barely walk but he could ride well enough despite the painful wound. His squadron had been assigned to guard three captured gendarmes that had been marched in the front of the column to further confuse any enemies. The order came that their usefulness was no longer needed, and with the ceasefire voided they were to be executed. Józef passed on the order to his men, who carried it out.

On the way to camp that night the 2nd squadron ambushed a German car and killed four SS men. A briefcase full of documents was captured.

On the 21st they ran into another band of RONA troops. Everyone prepared for another battle as the RONA command was asking to see documentation and orders from the Poles, who of course had no such papers. The partisans created enough of a story to avoid being attacked, and quickly moved on.

At Bialystok they camped and rested for three days while Pilch tried to make contacts and get some orders, but the large group of unknown soldiers started attracting too much attention from the local German authorities, so they moved out and kept heading towards Warsaw. It was decided that a lot of the civilian travelers should now be left behind to stay in the town of Bransk, rather than continue on with the military mission ahead.

Again they stopped for a three day break to try and get direct orders, and again had no luck. German observation once more got them moving out.

There was only the last leg of the trek left to complete but it was an impossible undertaking. They would have to cross the great Wisła (Vistula) River to get to the outskirts of Warsaw. All the bridges were heavily guarded by Nazi battalions, and these were not the retreating and disorganized groups they had been encountering, but well-armed and fortified units with intact command. This was not an area of chaos and advancing Russians, but a still fully controlled German occupation zone.

Pilch brought together his council of officers. "Gentlemen, we have a reckoning. We have a bridge crossing that appears impassable. We have no orders, and no contact with command whatsoever. It is an option to break our army apart and go our separate ways in small groups. Maybe some of us can sneak through and get to the city, find Home Army units, and help with the uprising. We will have to abandon most of our weapons and lose our organized structure. It will be the end of our journey together." He paused and looked each man in the eyes. "Or we decide to somehow stay together, try to cross the bridge at Nowy Dwór openly, through a German Army that has the approaches lined with troops and tanks."

Pilch then listened to his men with a growing sense of wonder and pride. The men discussed how much they had all gone through together. How they had been nearly destroyed twice, and how they had risen again from impossible hardships. They brought up all the losses of brave men and women, and how new heroic volunteers had rushed to join and fill up their ranks. And they discussed the powerful force they were in their current state. They were battle hardened, expert soldiers. They were exquisitely armed. They were organized, with infantry, cavalry, medical units, and fantastic commanders. This army can be of great service to Poland, they reasoned, just when it needs us the most.

They were not ready to give up.

Once again, the final decision after hearing everyone out was for Pilch to determine. He deliberated for a moment, but it was now a decision of the heart.

Sometimes strength of heart, rather than calculated odds, is what wins wars, he thought to himself. *This dedication and courage should not be curtailed.*

"We will attempt to cross the bridge together," he finally said. "Let's start forming a plan. And a backup plan in case things get hot."

Chapter Twenty-One

THE BRIDGE

ON A WARM SUNNY DAY at the end of July, the Stołpce-Naliboki group of the Home Army proceeded openly towards the bridge over the Wisła River at the town of Nowy Dwór. They began passing through more and more German troops as they plodded steadily along, drawing confused stares and bewilderment. But the openness and calmness of their approach seemed to imply some legitimacy. *A hostile Polish Army surely wouldn't march right into such a situation*, the enemy must have thought, as the Poles strode along unmolested. But the tension was high and increasing with every step.

They were finally stopped some distance from the bridge entrance by armed guards. As the column came to a halt, the wary Germans started up their tanks. The loud engines roared to life, then the tanks clattered into attack formation facing the Polish troops. Anxiety and palpable fear was as thick in the air as the summer heat. Local townspeople could be seen moving quickly out of range of an expected battle. Józef sent Franciszek Kosowicz along one side of the column while he trotted the other, quietly urging everyone to keep calm and not initiate anything unless attacked first. The backup plan entailed piles of hidden grenades and what would be a fight just for escape and survival. At such close contact there would be heavy losses on both sides, but the Poles would eventually be massacred by the vastly superior forces. They wanted to avoid any spark that would set off this powder keg.

Pilch had chosen four men to negotiate, and sent them forward. They were Franciszek Rybka, Aleksander Wolski, Franciszek Baumgart, and Stefan Andrzejewski. Each spoke German fluently. The German guards appeared totally perplexed by the approach of the unknown army.

The negotiation team walked up to the guards and began talking to them. The Poles at the front of the column could see the discussion under way, craning their necks and watching intently for hints as to which way this might go. One guard was seen shaking his head and the other guards stood with arms folded, while the Polish men tried to explain something. No progress seemed to be made and the column just stood in the hot sun near the entrance to the bridge. German soldiers peered at them suspiciously all along the line. Eventually the German guards seemed to get frustrated and turned to the bridge, waving the Polish men along to follow them. It was obvious no decision could be made without higher authority. A minute later the Polish delegation began discussions anew with two higher ranking German officers.

Rybka explained his story to them, that this army was obviously German allied, or how could they have traveled safely all this way? And one could see they had many German controlled Belarus police soldiers with them, demonstrating this fact clearly. The officer was in turn demanding written orders to clarify where they were going. Rybka explained in his perfect German that there were no documents due to the chaotic situation back east, but that all he had to do was contact the German garrison in Iwieniec, and they would confirm everything he was saying. Rybka of course knew the Russian front had already overtaken Iwieniec, and no Germans would be answering any phones, but was hoping the bluff would work. It did not.

The discussions continued with increasing impatience from the German lieutenant. The story seemed in some ways believable. It was truly inconceivable that this uniformed and impressive army could arrive here as an enemy from hundreds of kilometers away, all through occupied territory. But he was in no way ready to let them cross without more proof.

Meanwhile, another Wehrmacht army battalion arrived behind the Polish column. Both the Polish and German armies were now halted, standing in the hot sun, waiting at the bridge. The commander of the blocked German Army quickly became angry with the delay, and decided to ride past the Polish column in his staff car to see what the holdup was. As he was being driven along, he also looked with confusion at the strange Polish Army. He pulled up to the group of negotiators at the entrance and angrily demanded that the bridge crossings start moving. The bridge lieutenant explained the situation, leading to frustration all around. But Andrzejewski recognized the new officer immediately.

Andrzejewski had fought in the Prussian army in the First World War under Wilhelm. The arriving German officer was Major Von Jasten Valdan. He had been, by incredible coincidence, the commander of Andrzejewski's squadron. Andrzejewski clicked his heels and saluted his old leader with Prussian precision. The major was surprised to recognize his former sub-officer in this circumstance, and the two men shook hands in a heartfelt manner. The Poles watching from a distance were astonished to see what appeared to be a friendly greeting between the Pole and the German. *What is happening?* they thought as they turned to each other in bewilderment.

Andrzejewski took a moment to poetically reminisce to the major about some of their fellow soldiers, remembering especially some of their compatriots who had been killed in that previous war. The German officer was moved. Then Andrzejewski took it further in a burst of confidence bordering on reckless bravado. He began complaining about the treatment now occurring: that his men and horses had been standing in the hot sun for way too long, and that they should not only be passed through, but could use some supplies and accommodations once across. His former leader then turned impatiently to the German lieutenant and stated firmly, "This man is definitely who he says he is." The major then went on to demand that the bridge holdup should be moved along immediately, as his own battalion was also waiting too long in the heat, with desperate deadlines of their own.

The nervous Polish partisans watched with surprise as their three negotiators arrived back with perfectly calm, pleased faces. The column was waved through and crossed the bridge safely, passing by the numerous German soldiers who gazed at them still confused, but, by then, with an occasional wave or smile. Once across the bridge the

German garrison allowed them to stay in the nearby town of Dziekanów for three days, and, amazingly, supplied them with food and additional ammunition for their German weapons.

The winning battle of the 1920 Polish-Soviet war is remembered by the Poles as *"Cud nad Wisłą"*, or *"The Miracle on the Vistula."* Among the Partisans, the crossing was now being referred to as the *"Second Miracle on the Vistula."* As the story passed through the ranks it amazed everyone. How could this have happened? Did we really cross that bridge unharmed? With all our arms and soldiers, without a single shot?

Chapter Twenty-Two

KAMPINOS FOREST

DAYS LATER, AS EVENING FELL, they approached the outskirts of the Kampinos forest near Warsaw. The mist was rising in the lower meadows as the tired column walked along and entered the town. The moon made its appearance in the twilight, and a few street lights lit up and glowed softly. The large army, almost a thousand men in Polish uniforms not seen since 1939, bearing well-maintained weapons of every type, captured attention immediately. The rhythmic sound of hooves and wheels and the jangling of harnesses and equipment alerted the whole town to their arrival. They plodded along down the main street, the column coming out of the dark and mist and into the gentle light of the lamps and homes, so that one could just make out the white eagles and Polish insignia on their dark green khaki uniforms.

The partisans watched as more and more villagers ran out, only to stop yards away with mouths agape. "Are they ours?" people asked, worried, because there hadn't been any open Polish armies since the year of invasion.

The word "ghosts" was repeatedly heard by the soldiers from the gathering onlookers. The crowds, some tearfully, looked on as horse after horse passed by carrying row after row of fierce yet handsome young partisans. The soldiers dipped their hats and waved, but the crowds stayed largely quiet, just murmuring and staring.

Finally a boy of eight or nine, having heard the frightful analysis, daringly ran out and slapped a mounted soldier on the leg before turning away and shouting, "They're real!" to his astonished family. A dam was broken and cheers suddenly erupted from the crowds. Wave after wave ran up to the partisans to exuberantly re-enact the boy's move by slapping at the soldiers legs and sides, repeatedly exclaiming, "they're real, they're real, they're real!"

Women darted back into homes and reappeared with flowers or items of food and drink that they handed to the beaming soldiers. The scene turned into a joyful street party. The appearance of the mysterious ghost army caused a sensation, and word spread around the whole Kampinos region.

The next day, Adolf Pilch dressed in civilian clothes, borrowed a bicycle, and headed toward Warsaw to make contact with command, leaving his army in the welcoming town at the edge of Kampinos forest. He made his way inconspicuously down streets and alleys until reaching a known underground-affiliated cafe that he had been told about by AK, or *Armia Krajowa (Home Army),* members in the village.

By chance, he met up with someone he knew. It was a fellow Cichociemni parachutist who was able to help get him to the Home Army leaders. Pilch arrived at a secret headquarters in Warsaw looking for orders, but unfortunately, found a chilly reception.

A few kilometers away, Captain Józef Krzyczkowski sat at his desk in a house within the Kampinos forest. This 8th region was his area of command. He had a decent size force of roughly three hundred and fifty soldiers, and was tasked with fighting the Germans in this large and key area. The roads, towns, and farms would all be a factor in the upcoming uprising, as the Germans' free use of the assets here could benefit them greatly. Denying access to these assets was going to be important for the uprising. But how? He didn't have enough men for sure, but what he really lacked were weapons, ammo and experienced commanders. He looked over some papers absentmindedly and then neatly slid them off to the side. Then pulled out some maps, only to push them away also.

He placed his hands on his head and slumped forward in resignation. There was no solution. There were no arms to be had.

There were no more men to be had. He could not do what he was asked to do.

His adjutant walked in. "An army has arrived in Kampinos," he stated.

"What kind of army?" the surprised captain asked.

"An army of a thousand Polish partisans has arrived here in Kampinos. They came from the borderlands. They are experienced and battle trained. They arrived two days ago in full uniforms," explained the adjutant.

Krzyczkowski was incredulous. "What in the world are you talking about?"

"They are armed to the teeth and have wagons full of ammunition."

The Captain just sat stunned for a moment, blinking, and looking at the possibly confused adjutant.

"I need to see this for myself immediately, because I don't believe it," he said. "You will take me tomorrow to see them."

"There is a problem," said the adjutant.

"How could this possibly be a problem?" asked the captain.

"Their leader, a man named Pilch, is under investigation. Command is practically accusing him of being a traitor. The whole army may be sent away on a deadly mission to get rid of them. Seems he made a deal with the Germans without proper authority. There is a worry that this is some kind of Gestapo trick."

The captain's mood went from hopeful excitement to flat disappointment in an instant. "Tomorrow you head over and start interviewing them. Let's try to find out what they are all about," Krzyczkowski ordered.

The next day the captain was pacing and agitated about this strange development. He couldn't stand waiting for his assistant's report, so he dressed in a suit and rode his own bicycle to the camp of the mysterious partisans. When he arrived he found Pilch had gone to Warsaw to try and make contact with command. Krzyczkowski found second-in-command Rybka and arranged to speak to him privately. Rybka explained the whole history of the group, but the captain was skeptical. This was all too far-fetched and bizarre. The next day he received word from Major Kazimierz Krzyżak that the Stołpce-Naliboki group should be disarmed and Pilch put on trial.

"I cannot disarm this fierce army with my three hundred and fifty barely armed men," he replied. After further discussions, the decision was made to send the army away from Warsaw into enemy territory. It was a death sentence. Krzyczkowski explained this to Pilch.

Adolf Pilch seemed totally broken by this news. "I cannot follow this order, I cannot send these men to their death," he explained. "I have a better idea. Why don't you take over command of this army? Why can't we join you?"

This was what the captain had hoped for all along, but he still had to consult with command. With his third visit and negotiation, it was finally allowed, with the understanding that Krzyczkowski would assume total responsibility if the plan failed.

Pilch still had to go through a humiliating trial. Despite his recent promotions by Nowogródek command and his two iron cross medals, he was treated like a problem.

Pilch explained his actions clearly and without hesitation, emphasizing the desperate situation his men had faced, and how they had been at risk of complete annihilation. With confidence he laid out how decisions were made, and how his actions saved his army and their families. He also explained the near complete lack of orders and support, and how he had urgently tried to keep command aware of what was going on. Pilch had nothing to hide, and had no regrets.

It was ultimately decided that Pilch and the group would be given a chance to redeem themselves through service. Captain Krzyczkowski soon became an advocate for Pilch, and it was he who received the benefit, as the Stołpce-Naliboki group was combined with his existing forces to form the new "Kampinos group" of the Home Army. Krzyczkowski now had a much larger army, and it was suddenly extremely well supplied and armed. He liked and trusted Pilch going forward, and after hearing his whole story, made him his second-in-command.

Chapter Twenty-Three

THE FREE REPUBLIC

THERE WAS NO TIME FOR REST as the new army was quickly organized into its combined form. Pilch had found a fantastic quartermaster whose team did wonders acquiring food and supplies. Whole herds of cattle and loads of other goods were taken from German control in well organized ambushes and actions. Camps were set up and key locations taken over by the partisans. The uniforms of captured German gendarmes were appropriated and used by the partisans for stealthy raids and attacks.

The 27th cavalry stayed as it was with four squadrons under Nurkiewicz. Józef Niedźwiecki remained leader of the 2nd squadron. He now had over ninety soldiers under his command, divided into three platoons. When new alignments were being formed and volunteers moved around, Józef witnessed something remarkable. Not one of his men or women left his unit to join another. Despite a wealth of other good officers and opportunities, all his fighters chose to stay with the squadron. The unit had not only become one big family, but confidence and appreciation of his leadership was strong. They knew he looked out for their safety, never taking unnecessary risks, and they knew he was one of them. He didn't sit back and avoid danger, but led from the front. It was the proudest moment of his life.

It was directed that all previous *noms-de-guerre* were to be changed. It was well known the Russians back east had compromised the secret names. Pilch changed from *"Mountain"* to *"Valley."* First squadron leader Jan Jakubowski went from *"Oak"* to *"Wołodyjowski"*, a main character from the Sienkiewicz 'Trilogy'. Józef Niedźwiecki, known until then as Sergeant *"Gray,"* made an easy transition to what was already his nickname: *"Lawina,"* in Polish, or *"Avalanche"* in English.

On August 1, 1944, the Warsaw Uprising began, with an explosion of fighting in the central city. The partisans had arrived just in time for their role in Kampinos. Fighting in this forest region began immediately.

On August 2 the Kampinos group battled in Pieńków, killing twenty-six enemy and losing one. On the 3rd they fought a battle at Truskaw, and also launched a major attack on Warsaw's Bielanski Airport. Captain Krzyczkowski led a charge of mostly infantry soldiers but was unable to take the heavily guarded airfield. Polish losses were high with over fifty killed, but despite the failure a good result was achieved. German command, out of concern over more future attacks and a possible loss of the field, decided to destroy the airport themselves rather than continue with a constant defense, so its use was lost to them for the remainder of the war. Krzyczkowski suffered a serious injury and was taken to the partisan-controlled hospital in Łaski. He handed over command to Pilch.

Before sunrise on the 4th, Sergeant *Avalanche* was directed into action. It was one month and two days since he had been shot in the leg, narrowly avoiding amputation, but he was ready for battle. A German requisition unit had been spotted heading into Kampinos. The courier from Pilch relayed the message and layed out their route on a map. The 2nd cavalry would intercept and try to destroy them before they arrived at their target village. He moved out fast with one of his platoons, galloping hard as the first hints of sunrise lightened up the woodland byway. They only had to go a few kilometers to bisect the route the Germans were taking.

Avalanche arrived at the road near Lipków and turned his men in the direction of the soon to be oncoming vehicles. They trotted along, scouting out the terrain for a good ambush spot. The partisans employed many methods in their attacks, often using creative tricks or large diversions to catch the Germans by surprise, but Józef decided in this case to keep things simple. Simple, precise, and deadly.

They found a good bend in the road with the right sightlines and higher ground to one side. The trucks would have to slow down a bit at the turn. Then, they dragged a medium sized log across the road after the curve, so it would be noticed late. The horses were taken away and tied off. To the right, on the higher ground, he set up men with machine guns, including an RKM. To the rear, some distance back, he directed another group. They stayed on one side to avoid crossfire mishaps. One side would be enough. *Avalanche* explained the plan quickly and clearly, then finished with "On my opening shot, open fire boys."

The sound of rumbling engines was heard in the quiet woods long before the two camouflage-marked German trucks were spotted in the distance. They drove at high speed until hitting the bend in the road, where they slowed slightly. The partisans assessed the targets - three men in each truck cab, nine more seated in the back, their helmeted heads clearly visible, bobbing above the wood sideboards.

The first truck spotted the log in the road at the last moment and hit the brakes hard, skidding to a stop. The second truck, in danger of hitting the first, locked its wheels and stopped inches behind. Whether the enemy instantly recognized a trap didn't matter, as there was no time to react.

Avalanche was already standing up and firing his carbine at the driver of truck one. His first shots then unleashed a torrent of bullets from the RKM and hand held machine guns hiding in the woods. Both windshields and side windows were blown out immediately and the six cab occupants died in seconds. The back soldiers had ducked down but bullets were ripping through the side panels and several screamed out after being hit. One tumbled out the back of the second truck and tried to stumble off but was downed by the back group of partisans. Three of the Germans jumped off the far side and ran for the opposite woods. But the then advancing rear group targeted them successfully also. The shooting ended abruptly, so that only the sound of injured men groaning came from the back of one truck.

"Throw your weapons out," *Avalanche* shouted. From the back of the second truck the injured Germans tossed out their carbines.

"Come out one at a time with your hands up," came the next order from Józef, but he then directed one of his own men, "*Hawk, order them in German.*"

Four German soldiers slowly slid off the back of the truck. All were injured by bullet wounds or shrapnel. They were searched quickly and then field dressed for the worst of their wounds. Then they were put back on the one still usable truck. Ten Germans were killed in the attack with no losses or injuries for the platoon. One of the trucks was destroyed, but the other was gained for use by the partisans and driven back. Ten carbines and some machine guns with ammunition were part of the spoils.

A village in Kampinos was spared a surprise German attack and kept all their foods and goods, and perhaps their very lives.

The ride back was slow and peaceful. There wasn't much conversation, as was often the case after the violence of a battle. Mostly, the men retreated into their own thoughts as they trotted along in the pleasant summer woods. Józef could see one of his newer men looked shaken. He tried to think back and remember if the young man had actually killed anyone before, but couldn't be sure. Maybe this was the first time. He sidled his horse up closer and asked him if he was ok.

"Just feeling a little sick is all," responded the soldier.

"We will be back soon. When you eat something, you may feel better," Józef said. The soldier just nodded, but his face betrayed his convulsing emotions.

The other men clued into the situation. They had been through the same feelings and recognized what was going on.

"You did a good job today," Witold chimed in, "You did your duty."

"That's right," added Kazimierz, "don't forget, those Germans weren't invited here, but they came anyway to torment us, it's their fault, not ours." They rode along quietly for a bit.

"I hear Germany is a beautiful country," said the young soldier finally. "Why can't the Germans just stay home?" This brought a few laughs. The remainder of the ride home was quiet.

Within the next couple weeks, the large forest region began being referred to by locals as *"the Free Republic of Kampinos."* It was being cleared of German influence as every incursion by the enemy was swiftly dealt with.

On August 8th, the 2nd squadron was awoken at dawn to the sound of loud engines approaching their camp. They scrambled into defensive positions as a line of tanks burst through the distant underbrush and clanked ominously toward them. *Avalanche* immediately sent a messenger to *Valley* for help, as they were overmatched. The courier rode off hard, and Józef hoped he could bring help fast enough. The rider was a brave and faithful young man whose *nom-de-guerre* was *"Sweet Tree"* as in "sweet tree of Jesus." He was given the name because of his deep faith and piety. It was taken from the title of a haunting medieval hymn that is sung during Lent in Poland. The boy was a very reliable aid to his commander and respected by everyone. They were counting on him in that crucial moment.

Avalanche sent men crawling forward with Projector, Infantry, Anti Tank (PIAT) Mk I weapons, while machine gun fire was directed at the tanks. The lead tank was hit by a PIAT round from very close range in the thick underbrush and was disabled. Then a second tank was hit and began burning. The line of tanks paused their direct assault as German troops swarmed around looking for the PIAT crews. Some of the troops came under fire by the Polish machine guns and men began dropping. Tanks fired a few rounds at the Polish line causing terrific explosions that killed one man.

Sweet Tree arrived back in record time with the 1st squadron galloping behind. They sprang into action and started firing their three Model 35 anti-tank rifles at the attacking tanks. These giant long-barreled rifles had a super high velocity bullet that didn't actually penetrate armor, but the heavy impact caused shrapnel to break free in the interior of the tank, often injuring or killing crew members. The scary effect of this and the continued efforts of the PIAT crews had the surprising result of turning back the attack. The Germans, perhaps afraid of heavy losses for small gains, withdrew the offensive.

Supplies from the west were parachuted in on August 9. The most valuable arrivals included RKM machine guns, Smith & Wesson revolvers, and Sten machine guns. The Stens were quite popular, as they were short and light, even though they occasionally jammed after sustained fire.

Pilch was sending out the cavalry on frequent missions, usually at night. The directives were usually to hit two or three German holdings per outing, often at long distances apart. The Kampinos region was being cleared of the German Army completely, and the long distance runs and multiple actions gave the impression that the Poles had soldiers everywhere.

On the 13th, the 2nd squadron mounted an attack near Łaski, only to find the Germans gone. Alerted that a partisan troop was en route, they had fled. The Germans were starting to run scared in Kampinos, and what frightened them most was the quick-striking Polish cavalry squadrons.

After missing the fight at Łaski the squadron raced north, galloping hard to the next planned action. In the early morning they spotted a military vehicle raising a dust cloud in the distance. Through binoculars Józef spotted the German half-track. He gathered his men and quickly sent them off with their directives.

The half-track was motoring down the road when the driver suddenly spotted two uniformed Polish soldiers up ahead. The Poles seemed to react with surprise at the oncoming vehicle and spun around before wildly galloping into the woods to the left. One fired a shot at the Germans as he disappeared into the trees. The half-track pulled up to the spot and eased to a stop as the four German soldiers aimed their guns to the left and looked for the Polish riders. Stopping the vehicle was a fatal error. From the right, machine gun fire opened up and several grenades arched in. The explosions rocked the side of the vehicle and smoke enveloped the scene.

For the Poles attacking from the right, the half-track disappeared in the smoke cloud briefly, then was seen driving forward a few yards until the bare steel wheels sank into the ground. The grenades had broken the track so that it came apart in pieces when the vehicle moved ahead. Machine gun fire blazed out at the attackers from a small square window in the armored vehicle, and one of the Poles was hit as he stood up to shoot. Another German soldier jumped up and fired over the side before ducking back behind the heavy steel.

From the left, the two Polish riders had returned on foot, bounding unseen from tree to tree until close to the enemy. With all attention from the half-track now directed at the right, one of the two ran up to the side of the disabled truck and lobbed a grenade into the open back. The explosion ended the battle.

The following day Józef allowed his men to rest, but he made sure they spent the day cleaning their weapons and checking all of their equipment, as they did after every mission. He was saddened by the death of his soldier, taking personal responsibility. Thoughts of what he might have done differently preoccupied and tormented him. As he checked on his platoons he noticed one of his young men preparing his gear, and saw he was outfitted with a traditional saber attached to his belt. The men had mostly discarded the use of these, as they were unwieldy at times and didn't have much use in modern warfare. However, a few members still kept a saber in a scabbard attached to the saddle of their horses, strapped down out of the way.

"Why are you carrying that?" Józef asked.

The soldier looked a little embarrassed and just shrugged. "You can never have enough weapons I guess," he finally replied.

Józef was in no mood for games on this day, but thought about it for a moment before speaking. Being a member of the cavalry brought intense pride to these soldiers. Poland had a long and legendary history of cavalry going back to the Winged Hussars. From Grunwald to Vienna, to the Polish-Soviet War, it was the cavalry that won the historic battles. He knew the saber was an object of romantic pride for the young man, and that it helped him feel he was a part of that history. The boy was just a teenager.

"Ok, wear it. But don't fool around. Don't get carried away and start any duels, alright?" The young soldier, who went by the *nom-de-guerre "Zagloba"*, a comic hero from the Sienkiewicz 'Trilogy', nodded in agreement, relieved.

While continuing to check on his soldiers' work, Józef made note of their mental state. They were tired from the frequent night raids and intense fighting, but he could see contentment, even happiness on their faces. They were fighting for their homeland, and they were having success. They felt their work and sacrifice was a noble endeavor. The camaraderie and friendship they experienced added to the positivity. There was an expectation that they would all be recognized as great heroes after the war, and there would be parades and banquets in their honor. They would have beautiful wives and intensely proud children.

The long night raids and frequent actions continued. The appearance of several raiding parties in two or three different locations per night gave the Germans the impression that the Poles had a much larger force. Documents later showed that the German command estimated that there were over twenty thousand Polish troops in Kampinos, *ten times greater than the actual number.*

Pilch also sent out a special two-officer propaganda team. They traveled the region, leaving tidbits of exaggerated information about the size and strength of the Polish armies during their frequent stops, knowing the information would filter back to the Germans.

On one typical night the 2nd squadron headed out with *Avalanche* leading the first platoon. They rode hard until arriving at the first planned action, where they hoped to ambush a small German force staying near a village. They found no enemy at the location, but made a large commotion anyway, bursting into a few homes to search for enemy soldiers, and demanding any information on where they went. Then they apologized to the Polish citizens and loudly rode off, announcing that they were heading to the next town to the south.

Sergeant *Avalanche* took his troop a few kilometers east, and then took a sharp turn onto a logging road heading north. They rode hard again until exiting the woods onto a main road in a completely different locale, and turned east again. They crested a hill as the first hints of sunrise brightened the horizon, and looked at the next target below. It was a small building of dark colored logs and beams, nestled at the bottom of the hill. It was at the outskirts of a small town, and looked like a home, except for the telephone pole and wires that signified it was something more. Perhaps a post office or administration building in pre-war times.

A German staff car sat outside, facing up the hill towards them. The cabin was lit up and occupied. An SS soldier suddenly walked out and placed some boxes in the car. When he turned to head back in, he spotted the group of mounted partisans standing at the top of the hill just a short distance away. He ran inside while shouting. *Avalanche* instinctively reacted with a one-word command, "Charge!"

The spurred horses sprang down the short hill as three men ran out of the cabin and jumped in the car. One was wearing an SS officer's uniform and the other two were soldiers. They started up the roofless vehicle, but it was facing the oncoming rush. Józef was left behind as his fastest riders stretched ahead and closed the distance to the car. The vehicle jumped forward a few feet as the driver tried to make a sharp turn and escape, but it was too late, and the hard turned wheels caused the car to lurch and then stall.

The panicked soldier in the front seat lifted his MP-40 to shoot, but the first horseman was upon them already and fired a burst from his own Sten submachine gun, leaving a zig zag of bloody bullet holes across the driver and the gunner. The momentum carried the first horse past the car as *Zagloba* on the second horse followed a few lengths behind. In the back seat, the SS officer lunged forward and tried to gather up the gun from the dead man in front. The rest of the galloping cavalry watched as *Zagloba* seemed to struggle awkwardly for a second, then suddenly pulled out his saber, lifted it high, and struck the SS officer as he charged past. The officer slumped back dead in the seat as the rest of the horses all roared past the car.

The cavalry riders reigned their horses in and gathered in a loose group. Every astonished face was now turned towards *Zagloba*, who had such a penitent and sheepish expression, that there could be only one reaction. They all burst out laughing uproariously. It went on and on, as every return look at his face triggered renewed hilarity.

"My gun strap caught, I... I just did it... it just happened." *Zagloba* stammered out, looking at Józef. It was clear that the boy was expecting to be reprimanded.

A new round of laughter erupted.

"That was the greatest thing I have ever seen," said Kazimierz in his typical matter-of-fact drollness.

"I will tell my grandchildren about this. The charge of the Polish Hussaria!" added *Bohun*.

"An SS lieutenant! With a saber! Of all things!" another remarked.

Józef composed himself quickly, holding back a smile. "Let's get to work," he ordered.

The men went about gathering all the weapons and looking through the boxes of documents. Everything would be taken back to command. A few of the men approached Józef. "Should we dispose of the bodies?"

Józef looked at the car. The two dead soldiers were slumped forward in the front seat. The lieutenant lay back as if napping, except for a hideous angled saber wound that split the top of his head to his cheek.

"No, this is just the type of scene we want the enemy to stumble upon, leave everything as it is," he answered.

The next afternoon, Józef spotted two more of his youngest men strolling around with sabers dangling from their belts. He had to turn away and suppress a laugh before he reminded them also to be careful and not get too carried away.

God, I love these boys, Józef said to himself, and thought about how much their exuberance and spirit reminded him of his brother Jan. *Lord help me to lead them well,* he said to himself.

Chapter Twenty-Four

Pociecha

O<small>N THE</small> 14<small>TH AND</small> 15<small>TH</small> of August, 1944, the Kampinos group, by request from Warsaw, sent help to the ongoing fight in the city. Three battalions of infantry were sent to try and break into the old town. The cavalry and the CKM unit were ordered to stay in the Kampinos forest to continue the successful effort there.

Pilch's leadership and the experienced partisans had cleared the Nazi presence almost completely. The roads and towns were off limits to German troop travel and the people were living free of that terror. Any Nazi incursions were swiftly ambushed. The confident partisans held large meals together, well supplied with good food by the successful work of the quartermaster. On the anniversary of the *Miracle on the Vistula,* a large Mass was held for the partisans and locals by Father Hilary, and hymns rang out at many locations throughout the region.

Despite the extraordinary success, bureaucrats in command decided that Pilch was not highly ranked enough to lead such a large force. Major Alfons Kotowski, *"Okon"*, was sent in to take over leadership of the Kampinos group.

In the city of Warsaw the battles continued to rage. The insurgents would take buildings, blocks, and streets, but could not hold onto territory given the lack of equal weapons and ammo. A furious Hitler ordered the murder of the civilian population. He had the right men for the job, as the SS Dirlwanger Brigade and the SS RONA had arrived at Warsaw. Massacres of civilians began, and the brutality was of historic proportions.

RONA forces entered the Radium cancer hospital for women. They first robbed all the staff and looted the building. Then, they went on a rampage of gang rape and murder of staff and patients.

Rooms were set on fire and many patients burned alive. The one hundred and seventy persons murdered here were unfortunately just the start. RONA men continued emptying building after building in the Ochota district of Warsaw, murdering every man, women, and child. The victims were marched out of apartments and shot in mass executions. The properties were looted of all valuables, which the Russian Nazis loaded into wagons to keep for themselves. In Ochota alone, over ten thousand innocent civilians were murdered in the most brutal manner.

News of these war crimes filtered back to Kampinos, filling the partisans with rage and deadly motivation. Desperation to help the city grew, but getting in through the blockades was not a simple proposition. When allowed, some of the Kampinos group had snuck into Warsaw in small groups. It was difficult to make it into the city, but the Germans had placed some Hungarian troops as guards. The Hungarians were unenthusiastic Nazis and ended up being friendly to the Poles in Kampinos. They secretly allowed some travel back and forth until later being replaced by RONA men. The major attacks to gain entry into the city did not fare well.

At one point a Hungarian troop asked the partisans to return the favor, asking for safe passage through Kampinos. It was twenty soldiers escorting around two hundred Jewish men. Pilch allowed this with the condition that the Hungarians place all arms on a wagon to be guarded by the Poles during the passage. Pilch temporarily separated the Jewish men from the soldiers, fed them, and asked if they wanted to be freed of their guards and remain with the Polish group. Only a few did openly, but when the detachment left, a total of forty-six Jews had hidden and then returned to join the partisans. They were welcomed in and became soldiers, spread out into various detachments.

One of the Jewish men, Istvan Garami, became a professor and was interviewed many years later. He praised the Polish partisans highly, describing them as brave and very humane. He singled out Pilch as the best partisan commander he came across.

On August 22, the partisans attacked the Gdańsk train station. It was a heavily fortified location on the edge of Warsaw. The attack was planned out and directed by *Okon,* although he was not seen during the fight. On two successive nights, over seven hundred and fifty men were sent charging in against German machine guns and heavy weapons in concrete bunkers. During the attacks, Panzer trains with artillery were also rolled in to hammer the oncoming Poles. The partisans, so effective in the country and woods, had to cross eight hundred yards of open area with little cover. They didn't know the area and had no maps or guides. Despite incredible bravery in the attempt, the terribly flawed plan led to disaster. The Poles were decimated and suffered losses like never before. In two nights they lost four hundred and fifty men. It was an inconceivable tragedy, especially for the Stołpce-Naliboki men, who had come so far and been so careful with the lives of their soldiers. The lost men had been so willing to come to the aid of their beloved capital city, and many saw its skyline for the first time before dying at its edge on those two hellish nights.

The small number of exhausted men returned, covered in dust and blood, cut up from concrete rubble and ears ringing from explosions, only to be berated by *Okon* for their failure. They just didn't fight hard enough, according to their new commander. In a final humiliation, he demanded they turn over their weapons in order to send them into Warsaw. Some of the arms they carried had come directly from defeated enemies, and some had been carried and maintained since the

Iwieniec Uprising, but were to be taken away, as if to punish a naughty child.

Okon was off to a bad start with the Polish fighters, who were used to a different type and quality of leadership. The men maintained discipline, but a slow burn of anger and resentment was building.

The partisans had been incredibly successful in Kampinos, but pressures were building as the Germans began attempts to take back roads and towns. One key town at an important crossroads was Pociecha. The town was an area of particular focus because so many of the Kampinos Forest roads converged there. By controlling this outpost, the partisans would be able to block the best routes through the forest and cut off the Germans' access to the region. When Pilch received intelligence that the enemy planned to make moves on Pociecha, he sent the 3rd squadron to defend it.

Another looming threat was the German battalion from Nowy Dwór. When they had found out how badly they were fooled by the Poles crossing the bridge, they flew into a rage. They were more than eager to get back at the partisans for this humiliation, and were just waiting for the attack order.

RONA troops were sent in, arrived at Truskaw, and successfully occupied it. The Poles attacked immediately but could not dislodge the large number of enemy forces. A battle continued for days.

The expected confrontation at Pociecha materialized when the Germans attacked on August 31. Pilch sent *Avalanche* and the 2nd squadron to help defend it. He arrived to find a fight already underway and many buildings already burning, but was able to rescue a trapped patrol of scouts right away. He had his men dig in on the sandy berms of stunted pines that surrounded the crossroads. German infantry arrived in large numbers and cut off the access from where more Polish help could arrive. The RONA army began shelling the Polish defensive positions with artillery from the nearby Truskaw, which was just south of Pociecha. Planes and two tanks arrived as the battle ramped up. The 2nd squadron continued fighting from their positions on the hot and dry berms while getting bombarded. They suffered from incredible thirst and no food as there was no access to supply them during the intense fighting. They began calling it the new "Westerplatte" after the heroic Polish defense of that peninsula under bombardment in 1939.

Helena and her friend Barbara were fighting on the berms, dug in with the men. They couldn't be restrained to lesser activities after having been trained in weaponry, and with the need for all hands in the fight. The female fighters in the Polish cavalry earned an appropriate nickname - *"The Amazons."*

Helena manned a machine gun, laying down fire on approaching Germans and avoiding the artillery and mortar attacks as bravely as any man. The conditions were unbearable. All the soldiers' faces turned black from the smoke and dust. Their eyes looked huge and white against their darkened, sooty faces, giving the impression of a line of brooding owls. Complaints were nonexistent though, as the conditions could only be withstood with attempts at humor.

"I am frying like a potato pancake," one would exclaim during a break in fighting.

"If you buried an egg in this sand it would cook in one minute," another shouted out.

"Hey, Czesław, go ask the Nazis for some water, or this thirst is only going to make me even more unpleasant when they get close again."

They held the crossroads through a second day until help arrived from the CKM group and the 4th squadron, who broke through from another direction. The Germans were suffering greater casualties in the ongoing battle when Pilch and Nurkiewicz also arrived with reinforcements. It was then that the enemy tried a last ditch attack by circling around and sneaking through the nearby wheatfields. The Poles prepared well, waiting for the Germans to get close, then surprising them with an all-out cavalry charge. The bold move panicked the oncoming forces who turned and bolted. The battle ended in a rout with over one hundred enemy killed and the German Hauptmann being captured.

The aftermath of the huge battle was a scene of devastation, with craters and blown-apart trees on the berms and much of the town burning. *Avalanche* lost two of his men, and the other Polish units lost a dozen more. Over thirty were injured. The Poles held the crossroads and the town, which kept the main roads inaccessible to the enemy. Major Kotowski congratulated Nurkiewicz on a great victory for the 27th cavalry.

The 3rd cavalry squadron arrived to relieve the 2nd in the aftermath of the main battle. During the lull in action Józef Niedźwiecki and Kazimierz Jankowski were gathering up the unit in preparation to leave. As they stood together on a berm they noticed the grouped horses began to fidget.

"Something is up," said Kazimierz, as they started looking around. Suddenly the horses pinned their ears back and showed more alarm.

"Everyone take cover!" Józef yelled as he ran among the two squadrons. An artillery shell exploded, sending a geyser of sand and pine branches high into the air and onto some of the men. A barrage commenced, forcing the 2nd squadron to dig in and wait longer before leaving for their desperately needed rest.

The RONA troops still held Truskaw and Marianów and were using the locations for their artillery to continue shelling Polish positions. The murderous SS men had been sent from the slaughter in Warsaw to start eliminating the Polish partisans, and now had toeholds in Kampinos. They were, after all, anti-partisan specialists.

Pilch felt an urgency to attack the RONA forces and eliminate their base of operations. He described it as his "soldier's intuition, which had never been wrong" that they should be attacked that very night. He went and proposed the plan to Kotowski, who initially refused. But Pilch was determined.

The SS RONA must be destroyed tonight, he felt with an overpowering conviction, as he went back to the major. The ongoing several-day battle must be ended decisively, and the time was now, he explained. The surprise night attack on Truskaw was finally agreed to, and a follow up action for Marianów the next night. Pilch's determination had convinced Kotowski.

A partisan known by the *nom-de-guerre "Sosna"* was sent to scout out the enemy positions, and he returned with very precise information. The same was done for Marianów by another partisan known as *"Dombrowa."* Pilch picked eighty men and led the action himself. At one in the morning they approached the town carrying only automatic weapons, pistols, and grenades. They entered the village, which had been emptied of its inhabitants, and began the attack on the street housing over five hundred RONA soldiers. At the first shots several local women who had been kidnapped ran out of the buildings and were directed by Pilch to hide in the woods. The partisans charged in, gunning down enemy soldiers and throwing grenades into cellar windows. The SS men were caught completely by surprise and were slaughtered en masse. Over two hundred and fifty were killed. The artillery pieces were destroyed. Some prisoners were captured, but when the Poles found wagon after wagon of stolen loot from Warsaw victims, the prisoners were executed. Ten Polish men were killed in the battle.

Chapter Twenty-Five

Marianów

The attacks on September 3rd and 4th at Marianów were undertaken by sixty volunteers from Józef's 2nd cavalry squadron and the CKM squadron under *"Tom."* The men rode out into the night and stopped two kilometers north of the small hamlet, where they dismounted and left the horses with holders.

The order was given out to maintain strict silence. Not a word, not a cough, not a heavy footstep was to be heard until the signal for battle. They began following their scout in careful and quiet single file as they headed south through the night woods. Step by step they had to snake a path through mined areas that protected the approaches to the town. It was a painfully slow, tedious process. They took a wide route to the right and circled around in silent procession until they were approaching the occupied town from the south. Marianów was at the southern edge of Kampinos forest.

Towns further south were German controlled and held no partisans. Scouting had found that the southern approach was unprotected and unguarded by sentries. RONA never expected the possibility of attack from the rear, so all their artillery and attention focused to the north, where the partisans resided.

By three in the morning the volunteers were lining up in attack formation just south of the RONA occupied houses. *Avalanche* and *Tom* checked the line quietly, then settled into their own predetermined locations. There were about a dozen buildings to hit, and each had its assigned team.

It was dead quiet and absolutely still as the men crouched or lay prone just a short run from the line of houses. Józef looked at *Tom* and nodded. *Tom* sent a hand signal to his man who carried the flare gun that would signal the start of the charge. The soldier stood up and fired the gun into the sky. The whole line was tense and on edge, so the instant the sound of the flare gun was heard, everyone leaped forward and started firing before the flare even exploded in the sky above.

After hours of silence the sudden ear-splitting sound of machine guns and grenade explosions shocked the system, and Józef stumbled as he jumped up and charged. He righted himself and ran hard at his building, carrying his German submachine gun. He targeted the building the scouts had said housed many of the officers. His man *Bohun* followed him. Reaching the building, Józef leaped onto the porch and slid up next to the door, his back against the wall. He watched *Bohun* kick out a cellar window and toss in a grenade, which exploded seconds later sending flames out the broken window. *Bohun* ran up to join Józef at the door, and Józef unlatched it from the side and swung it open.

Gunfire erupted from inside, splintering the wooden door frame. Józef rolled in a grenade and slid back against the wall as it exploded. He was conscious of the sound of a heavy battle raging all around as he stepped into the dark smoky room and opened fire with his machine gun. He could not see a thing in the blackness and smoke but sprayed back and forth until the magazine clicked empty. Standing in the pitch black, he listened as he started to choke on the smoke.

The sound of the surrounding battle could be heard: explosions, machine gun bursts, and the screaming of men and panicked horses. Józef then heard movement from inside. A couple of shuffled steps, then a cough, then a weapon bolted back, then a whisper in Russian. Suddenly a burst of fire opened up from inside the room and hit the wall to the side of his head.

Józef quickly crouched low and pulled his pistol. He had seen the flashes of the gun but now could hear that men were moving in the dark. He reached for the door, planning to escape back out, but to his shock the door had closed and wouldn't open. He couldn't get out. He slumped down into a sitting position and strained to make out where the enemy was. They were looking and listening for each other in a blind standoff.

Outside, flames were rising high in surrounding buildings. A few faint shafts of light bounced across the smoky room. For just a fraction of a second, Józef saw three silhouettes illuminated on one side before it went dark again. Men with guns, looking for him, spread out across the room. Józef lifted the pistol, held it in front of his chest and opened fire at the invisible enemy, going left to right, emptying his gun at the spots where he had seen them. He heard a grunt and the sound of bodies falling as he jumped up and hit the door hard with his shoulder. It opened halfway and he tumbled out, gasping for air.

Bohun had been hit by gun fire and killed, and had slumped against the door, causing it to seem locked. Józef tossed his last grenade back through the door and ran around the house to the street as it exploded. He snapped another magazine in his machine gun just in time to see two armed RONA men running out from a building across the way. He dropped them both with two short bursts.

A second flare shot into the air above signaled the Poles to move out. To both left and right he could see his fellow partisans walking forward in a loose line. They were passing through the town at a steady pace, still searching for enemies. Every building was by then in full burn, and the firing became more sporadic as they ran out of targets. Russian shouting and screaming could be heard amidst the gunfire and the crackling and whistling of raging fires.

The Poles made their way past the last few houses and exited the town. The action had taken less than thirty minutes. They continued north into the woods and then found the scout waiting to escort them back around the mined areas. The SS men still alive in Marianów were so thoroughly shocked and confused that they were still firing weapons and shouting, even though the attackers had long gone and were now some distance away. Perhaps in the chaos and destruction they were shooting at shadows, or even at their own men. The results of the attack were later estimated to be around one hundred enemy killed and twenty injured. The Poles lost three men.

The two night attacks on RONA were devastating for the enemy. Their heavy losses left them unable to continue as a unit in Kampinos, and German command disbanded the failed battalion shortly after the disastrous nights in Truskaw and Marianów. The SS RONA, having been sent to Kampinos to destroy the Polish resistance, was instead destroyed by the partisans.

The RONA leader Bronislaw Kaminski was later executed by the Germans, although they tried to frame it as a partisan assassination. It happened to occur that in the hundreds of rapes the diabolical group had committed they had victimized two German girls, infuriating the powers that be. In addition, the German command was frustrated with the overall behavior of the unit. It wasn't the rape, murder, and pillaging of goods that bothered command so much as the fact that these activities often took precedence, and kept the RONA Brigade from meeting military objectives.

Chapter Twenty-Six

THE BAD AND THE GOOD

DESPITE THESE GREAT military successes, the Kampinos group suffered a huge blow to morale and to their numbers with the desertion of Captain Dulka. He was a leader from the local Kampinos men before the arrival of the Stołpce-Naliboki army. While engaging his men in battle, the flyover of a German reconnaissance plane caused him to panic. Against orders he stopped the attack and retreated. Convinced that the Germans would send in a large force and destroy his battalion, he inexplicably told his men that they had no chance, and should give up and go home. Most of his men followed his order and abandoned the Kampinos group. Approximately three hundred stayed and moved over to Pilch.

With the huge death toll from the Gdansk train station attack and then the desertion of Dulka's men, the Kampinos group suddenly was down to only fourteen hundred soldiers. They had been over twenty-six hundred at their peak, just a short time ago. The main force was now largely made up of former Stołpce-Naliboki soldiers and officers.

There was a great danger that the Nazi forces arrayed around Kampinos might discover the actual size of the Polish forces. Pilch moved to make sure all entry roads were well guarded, and positions fortified. The raids against any enemy presence continued as before, so no change would be noticed.

Major Kotowski, *Okon*, continued with his heavy-handed style of leadership. He enforced strict discipline over relatively unimportant things, and gave out tasks impossible to complete. He did not take his officers recommendations with respect, overruling them dismissively. After suffering heavy criticism from above for the loss of life at the train station, he seemed to take out his humiliation on his underlings, blaming them.

There were rumblings of discontent among the soldiers and officers. They were shocked by this treatment, having been used to a different approach. Kotowski's fits of anger and abuse seemed to be getting worse. When *Okon* pulled his pistol out and threatened his own men with the words, "I will shoot you like dogs," some officers decided to go visit Captain Krzyczkowski in the hospital and demand he reign *Okon* in. The Captain called Kotowski for a meeting, but the major never went.

On September 7th, Pilch led an attack on a German unit guarding a bridge construction project. Thirty enemy soldiers were killed and the bridge construction ended. Battles occurred also on the 13th at Mariew, back at Pociecha on the 16th and 17th, and on the 21st at Polesie Nowe.

Józef made time to visit some of his injured men at the hospital in Łaski. One of the chaplains to the partisans was stationed here, and he was proving to be not only a holy man, but a courageous one also. He went by the *nom-de-guerre "Radwan 3."*

On one occasion *Radwan* had heard about a German ambush being planned, and was able to rush out and warn the incoming partisans. They avoided the attack and were saved. He later found an injured partisan girl in the forest who had lost a lot of blood, and carried her for two kilometers to the hospital, where she survived. He even assisted doctors in surgery when they were short-handed. He was providing strong spiritual and administrative help to the partisan-controlled hospital and the region in general. The hospitalized men told Józef of this chaplain's great care and compassion. One relayed a story:

"*Radwan* sat and talked to me for a long time. He is a good man, and he has a lot of charisma. We talked about how Poland can possibly survive all this suffering. He told me that he was standing on a hill overlooking the fires in Warsaw, praying, and the hot winds carried a piece of charred paper that landed at his feet. He picked it up and on it were the words *'Thou shalt love'*. It was a profound message from the burning capital, he said. It was quite a moving thing to hear."

Józef sat silently with no reply. He couldn't wrap his head around such spiritual ideas, given all the blood, gore, and violence he was living. *There will be a time for love someday*, he thought to himself, *and for goodness, and for compassion, and maybe even mercy, but not now.*

He left his men, hoping they would recover from their serious injuries. On the way out he met *Radwan*, who was walking in, and thanked him for the care of his men. The priest thanked Józef in return for his service to Poland. They chatted for a few moments. Józef felt the urge to talk with the priest longer, there were so many concerns occupying his mind, but a nurse interrupted asking for *Radwan* to come quickly for a patient. The perceptive priest looked at Józef with concern, realizing that he needed to talk, but the nurse urged the chaplain to hurry. Józef stood still for a moment then went back to his squadron.

Radwan 3, whose real name was Stefan Wyszyński, went on to great fame. He became a bishop and then a cardinal, then the primate of all Poland. He bravely resisted the communists as leader of the Church in Poland, even suffering through an imprisonment, which he bore with fortitude and bravery. He mentored and shepherded a young priest named Karol Wojtyla through his own rise through the Church, and in 1978 was there in Rome to be embraced by the new Polish Pope.

The Warsaw Uprising had a political purpose. The Polish nation wanted to show the world that it was still there, and that it was liberating its capital city for its own Polish independence. It had been crucial to start the uprising before the Soviets arrived to claim Warsaw. What no one expected was that the Red Army would stop at the Wisła River, and sit idle while watching the Germans destroy the city and massacre the population. The Russians even denied air space for Allied planes to provide relief and supplies. The uprising was slowly choked out and defeated.

The Nazi war machine now turned its focus onto the Kampinos forest. The roads and towns of this important region needed to be regained for use as the dual fronts closed in on the Reich. With the uprising squashed, Germany now had the troops freed up and available to destroy the partisans. They called the plan *"Operation Sternschnuppe," (Operation Falling Star)*.

General Vormann worried that the Red Army would link up with the Kampinos group and then cut off the SS units near Modlin. He planned to eliminate this possibility by defeating the Poles well before this could happen. On September 27th the operation began with over five thousand troops supported by planes and tanks and other armored vehicles.

Heavy bombardment drove the partisans out of their defensive positions at Wiersze and Brzozówka, convincing Major Kotowski to prematurely order a massive retreat of all forces. He started them on a long march, hoping to escape south to the Holy Cross mountains.

It was the second night on the march and Sergeant *Avalanche* was leading his squadron, riding at the head of his 1st and 2nd platoons. His 3rd platoon was up ahead scouting the path. Józef stopped his men, and signaled the platoon leaders to join him. The courier *Sweet Tree* was sent to halt the 3rd platoon also. Morning was approaching and the men and horses needed a rest. As soon as the order was given, men dismounted, found a dry spot, and went to sleep.

Sleeping wasn't an option for their commander though, as Józef was too concerned about the current predicament.

The Russian front was only fifty miles away, and yet things had become strangely quiet. The Poles suspected that Stalin was holding back and allowing the Germans to destroy the Polish Resistance. A large German force was free to array against them, and was already on their trail.

His thoughts were interrupted by two fast approaching figures. They were boys from the 3rd platoon. "Enemy patrol heading this way," they reported, "Platoon leader is letting them pass."

Józef promptly ordered the 1st platoon awake and into action, and had them form a semicircle on the edge of the woods. Then he had the 2nd platoon provide cover with its machine guns. They waited silently as the German patrol appeared and walked straight into the trap. The Poles quickly closed in on them, shocking them completely. The 3rd platoon that had let them pass entered the clearing and closed the circle. The horrified enemy raised their hands in surrender. It was a troop of seventeen men, including two sergeants. The partisans quickly stripped them of their weapons, and Józef walked up to question the sergeants. They had thought that their mission was routine, he learned, and did not expect any partisans in this area, especially since they had large forces not far away.

Józef sent his courier out again, to report the capture to the main column some distance back. Intelligence officers arrived quickly and interrogated the Germans further, then told *Avalanche* that the prisoners were at his disposal, and to use his judgment on what to do with them.

This was a dilemma. Dragging prisoners along in the current situation was out of the question. The journey was already too difficult and dangerous. Setting them free was also a problem. They could possibly return to their base and supply information before the Poles could clear the area. There was another factor. His men had all suffered terribly under German occupation. Everyone had lost friends or family members. Partisans in particular were rarely shown any mercy when captured, and often were tortured before being killed.

His soldiers were more than ready to eliminate a group of hated enemies. He could see it in the hard, determined expressions on his men's faces. Certainly if these captives were SS men they would remain in the forest forever, but these were regular Wehrmacht. The prisoners, all young men just like his own, looked at Józef with burning, pleading eyes, knowing he held the power of life and death over them. For Józef, all the years of internal struggles seemed to crystalize into this moment. What to do with this brief, but incredible power? He looked them over silently.

A strong feeling overcame him at this moment. *What are we fighting for, if we are to become like our enemy? I must remain true to myself. I must keep a clear conscience,* he thought to himself as he made his decision.

"Prisoners, you are free to go," he finally ordered.

Hesitatingly at first, the Germans started to walk away, but looked back over their shoulders as if they expected a sudden volley of bullets. The two sergeants stared at Józef's face as they moved off, then turned away for the last time and disappeared into the misty early morning woods.

Józef ignored the few unhappy glances he received from his men, but no one questioned his authority. The troop began their journey again, hoping to continue on to a safer locale.

Chapter Twenty-Seven

Jaktorów

THE NEXT DAY, THE POLISH ARMY was approaching the town of Jaktorów when Major Kotowski called for a halt to rest the men and horses. They were truly exhausted, but Pilch and the other officers urged *Okon* to keep moving a few more hours until past the nearby train tracks, which were elevated in height above the surrounding terrain. It would be good to get past the obstruction, and scouts reported that the area was currently lightly guarded. They could break through easily.

True to form, *Okon* refused all advice. They stopped moving and rested in place. Kotowski also wanted the trailing units to catch up to the main army and consolidate. The column had been more than a kilometer long, so it had to spread out in a large area. The front units settled on the flat field nearest the railroad tracks, and the rest in the nearby town.

A German Focke-Wulf 189 reconnaissance plane appeared and circled around the camp. The Poles were now spotted and their exact positions known to the enemy. The plane returned and started strafing the resting men, causing extensive damage and panicking the horses. Its recurrent passes destroyed some wagons and equipment and killed some men. The partisans opened fire on the plane with regular rifles and machine guns, usually a futile endeavor. Remarkably, it was hit, started smoking, and then crashed off in the distance, bringing cheers from the men. A short time later the units farthest back came under attack by German armored cars, and had to fight them off as they moved forward to escape.

The sound of fighting in the rear caused confusion among the partisans, who were not getting any orders to move forward nor go back to help with the battle. In fact, no orders came at all as they tensely waited. The other officers kept urging for some action, but *Okon* seemed frozen, and it wasn't until noon that he laid out his directives. They would move south and cross the tracks in two separate groups.

They began to move forward, engaging a now fast-increasing German presence. The most forward groups drove the Germans back from the railway, and a few Polish troops actually crossed the tracks before disaster struck. From the direction of Żyrardów, an armored Panzer train with forty armored cars rolled down the tracks, then stopped with a heavy screeching of its brakes. The Poles watched helplessly as it blocked the escape route. The heavily armed train began laying down withering artillery and machine gun fire. The forward groups on the flat plain were devastated and pinned down. Within minutes the area near the tracks was turned into a death zone of stripped clean saplings and craters. German infantry arrived in force and dug in all along the tracks. The Poles had to crawl back in retreat. They were being effectively surrounded, as German armored units approached from the rear and sides.

The Poles then had to fight a defensive battle against the encirclement, while being pounded by artillery, planes, and the oncoming tanks. They formed a defensive line in the shape of a quadrangle, using any natural barriers for cover.

The only hope was to hold out until night and then try to break through the lines either in force or in small groups.

Józef had his squadron take cover in two long irrigation ditches. They prepared for the grim task of a long battle against superior weapons. He took a position behind a large haystack where he could see both his lines but remain hidden from enemy fire. The intense fighting continued well into the afternoon. His men did wonders with the PIAT, a bazooka-like weapon, crawling far out from the ditches and disabling tanks before they could get close. But the artillery and bombing were taking a toll and he lost some men.

It was a clear day so the Luftwaffe was flying non-stop. The Poles were starting to run low on ammo as the afternoon dragged on. Józef had his men get mentally prepared for the fixing of bayonets, if it came to that. After dark they would try to charge through the lines both on horse and on foot.

Major Kotowski was last seen walking towards the rear. It was the last time he was seen alive. Orders finally came from Pilch, as he stepped up to remedy the void in leadership. After dark the partisans were to charge out through the lines in any direction possible, and regroup later some distance away. It was a last ditch and desperate plan for survival.

Suddenly everything went quiet around the battlefield. The Germans seemed to halt or pull back momentarily. Something big was brewing. A foreboding feeling came upon the men like a chill wind.

Józef called over *Sweet Tree*, and gave him the final orders to relay along the lines. He watched as his reliable courier alternately ran and crawled along the ditches. That's when the bomb blast exploded next to his haystack.

It was after dark when his eyes started flickering open. Water was being sprinkled on his face by someone kneeling at his side. He focused and saw it was none other than the *Sweet Tree of Jesus*.

Of course it is, Józef thought to himself. He tried to sit up but could not move yet. His body felt like concrete. "What happened?" he asked in a raspy voice.

"An explosion hit your spot and you went flying. The bombings seemed to be the signal for an all-out attack, because everything came at once. Artillery opened up and tanks and infantry moved toward us in great numbers. When they got near, our men all ran out and attacked the enemy."

Sweet Tree, now choked with emotion, paused, and then went on with a quaking voice. "Our boys bravely charged, and many were shot down. Some of them had run out of ammo and ran out with bayonets. When the advancing SS soldiers saw those bayonets coming, some of them panicked and ran away, dropping weapons that our men then picked up and used against them." The boy sobbed for a second before gaining control again. "I dragged you into the ditch, and seeing you were still alive, resolved to stay with you."

He began tearing up once more, and went on, "I saw *Zagloba* get killed, and Sowinski, and Cichy, when they charged. And that's not all - an hour ago, off in the distance, I saw the SS shoot some of our captured men in cold blood."

Sweet Tree again composed himself. "I think some broke out though. Kosowicz charged the line on horseback with some others. They threw grenades down as they leaped over and through the German soldiers and just kept going, being fired at all the while. Many fell there also, but not all. I will never forget the sight! It was such a daring and reckless charge, but it was the only way out."

Józef felt tears streaming down his own cheeks as he listened and heard about his boys. *How many have I lost?* he agonized.

"Did you see Helena?" Józef asked.

"No, I don't know what happened to her," replied *Sweet Tree*.

Józef sat up painfully. "Maybe we can find our way out on foot," he eventually said. "We have been in tight spots before, let's not give up hope."

With great effort and help from *Sweet Tree*, he got up and they began moving. The sounds of battle had died down. Only occasional shooting could be heard. They crawled through an empty potato field until they heard German voices. They backtracked and tried another direction. Again they came upon enemy soldiers. Over and over they walked or crawled some distance only to find the path blocked by roaming Germans.

Buildings and trees were on fire, casting light into the woods and fields, which made any possible escape all the more difficult. Occasionally a flare went off in the night sky, as the Germans were actively searching the area for any remaining partisans. It appeared all avenues of escape had abandoned them.

Exhaustion and pain was sapping all hope from Józef as futile hours of effort passed. He felt like just shutting his eyes and giving up. But after resting a few moments, he thought about his faithful companion, and feeling responsible for his welfare, he summoned the strength to keep trying.

They continued moving the whole night with no success, then finally hid in some dense undergrowth as morning came. "Maybe the Germans will leave the area, and we won't be spotted," he told his courier.

When the dawn broke on the battlegrounds, this hope was shattered. The Germans seemed to be everywhere, and were searching the grounds. They were going to be found, then probably tortured for information before being killed, Józef knew. Partisans had an alternative option though.

Józef pulled his pistol. "You know what we should do," he said to *Sweet Tree*.

The young man looked back at him with sadness and regret, and nodded. But a moment later he responded, "It's a sin I cannot commit, but if it's your order, you will have to do it. Just let me pray for a minute first." And then he began by turning away, dropping to his knees, and bowing his head, "Father in heaven, please forgive me for all my sins, Jesus, have mercy on me."

Józef felt his heart being squeezed and a lump formed in his throat. He could never harm this young man. He remembered the NKVD prison and the death march and the unlikely escape, and then all the other close calls and hopeless situations. He was still alive because he had kept his will to live.

Józef put his hand on the boy's shoulder. "Let's keep trying," he said. "Maybe there is a chance. If we get swept up by regular army, maybe we will survive somehow." He left it unsaid what would happen if they fell into the hands of the SS or Gestapo.

They sat still, waiting. First they heard the German voices getting nearer. They could then see the line of soldiers spread out, methodically moving towards them, searching everything in their path. There was no escape. Józef decided to surrender openly rather than risk getting shot by a surprised soldier. He and *Sweet Tree* stood up and raised their hands high. They were quickly and roughly set upon, pushed out into the open and marched off. Hard thrusts from the butt of a rifle to their backs and shoulders prodded them forward as they stumbled along the hellish battlefield of destroyed trees and blackened ground.

After a short walk, Józef's heart sank in terrible shock and disappointment. They were being marched right into the camp of an SS panzer division.

A tall good looking SS officer spotted the incoming prisoners immediately and strode over with purpose. His first action was to strike Józef hard in the face. Completely weakened from the blast injury and the long night, Józef was knocked to the ground by the blow. The officer then kicked him hard in the ribs. Bitterness and anger flowed through Józef's mind. After all that had happened, all the close calls and miracle escapes, *what a way to die, at the hands of a sick and twisted enemy, on the ground like a dog,* he thought.

He looked at the officer. The man was furious and in a rage, his face contorted with hate. Why?

Then it came to him. *We gave him a hell of a fight yesterday. He probably lost a lot of equipment and men.* Pride swelled up and Józef felt ready to at least die like a man, so he looked back at the officer with as much contempt as he could muster, locking eyes in a cold stare. The officer looked ready to explode. He kicked Józef hard again, and then pulled his pistol. Józef winced from the painful kick, and waited for the shot with his eyes closed.

Instead of a pistol shot he heard the sound of heels clicking together.

"*Herr Oberhauptsturmfure!*" someone said loudly. "We have to intervene."

Józef blinked out the tears from the last kick and focused on the two men who had just walked up. He recognized them. It was the two German sergeants from the captured night patrol. They were engaged with the SS Officer.

"We recognize this partisan commander as the one that took us prisoner yesterday, and then ordered our release. He treated us with proper military respect. He and his man were captured by the Wehrmacht, not the SS, so we will take charge of them."

The SS officer looked at them coldly. "We kill these Polish bandits wherever we find them," he said.

"Not these two" said the sergeant, matching the SS man's gaze.

Józef's mind could barely grasp the situation. Was he hallucinating? He felt as if God's hands were upon him, and all the pain left his body as he watched, transfixed. *Lord, if this is really happening, let me live a life worthy of your grace,* he said to himself.

The sergeant went on, "With respect, Sir, these prisoners are ours, and were mistakenly brought here, so we will take them off your hands. We are veteran officers, and are ready to take this issue to the division commander if necessary."

The SS officer stood for a moment, then just dismissively waved them off before angrily walking away.

The sergeants ordered their men to help Józef up and take him and *Sweet Tree* away. The Germans and Józef made eye contact one last time and gave each other a nod, before parting.

Józef and his courier *Sweet Tree* were taken by the Wehrmacht to a holding area, then loaded on trucks as prisoners of war. Józef, exhausted, struggled to stay seated and upright as the truck bounced along the road. He relived the moments of this miracle rescue in his mind over and over again, just as he would frequently for the rest of his life. They were taken on a long journey to Stalag XB near Bremen, Germany. They survived in difficult but not deadly conditions for the last months of the war. In April of 1945 the camp was liberated by British forces.

Chapter Twenty-Eight

HELENA

HELENA FIRED HER WEAPON until out of ammunition. When the first wave left the ditches to charge through the lines, she saw them get wiped out by enemy fire. She decided to move laterally and try to find a safer path. As she ran to the right she spotted a younger boy from the infantry who was still crouched in the ditch hiding.

"They are coming," she yelled, and waved for him to follow her. For several hours they carefully alternated running and hiding from German troops. As they hid along the wall of an abandoned house, the boy spotted the entrance to a root cellar.

"Maybe we should hide in here," he said, pulling open the wooden cover over the entrance. The exhausted Helena agreed, so they quickly threw some tree limbs and branches over the entrance, then cracked it open just wide enough to slide through and down.

It wasn't a big space, and was piled high with potatoes. Once they pulled the cover back in place it was pitch dark. They hid out for two days. During each day a small amount of light filtered in, and they could hear the sounds above as vehicles and German voices came and went. The waiting was torturous and Helena started having trouble breathing in the damp, moldy air of the cellar. They sat or reclined uncomfortably on the piles of potatoes.

After the second day it quieted down. They finally pulled back the cover and poked their heads out to look around. It seemed clear of soldiers, but they waited until dusk to emerge and walk around. They headed out towards the south in the dark of night. Helena was now very sick with a lung infection and fever. Her tongue got stiff and she could not speak. They approached a house in the woods where a kind woman took them in. She cared for Helena, helping her get bathed and then gave her medicine.

After a few days' rest, they had to go into the nearby town to get food. A German patrol entered the town and Helena, too weak to make a run for it, was caught in a roundup. She was held for two months in a local prison, then transferred to Ravensbrück Concentration Camp. She was forced into demanding and difficult work in the awful place until the Russian front drew near and the Germans moved the prisoners further away to another camp. When the war ended the Swedish Red Cross took over the camp. In May, the Red Cross moved the survivors to Sweden.

The fighting at Jaktorów was the largest partisan battle of World War II. The Poles suffered heavy losses. At least one hundred fifty men were killed, one hundred twenty wounded, and another one hundred fifty taken prisoner. The Kampinos group was effectively destroyed and ceased to exist.

Approximately two hundred soldiers were able to break out and escape the battle after a last ditch charge through the lines. Some found refuge with local townspeople. Adolf Pilch continued leading a small remnant of the partisan army until the end of the war.

Chapter Twenty-Nine

Postscript

JÓZEF NIEDŹWIECKI SURVIVED the POW camp and after the war joined fellow Polish soldiers in Italy. Eventually they were transferred to England, where the Polish Army men continued to draw a salary while waiting for the political situation to finalize. The Allied agreement at Yalta had betrayed the Polish nation and allowed it to fall under Soviet influence. Once sham elections were completed by the communists, the chance for Polish freedom evaporated. Józef realized he could not go home. The Polish heroes of the underground that remained in Poland were marked for persecution by the new communist regime.

While stationed in England, Józef searched the Red Cross lists of survivors and refugees. To his great joy he finally found Helena's name among the living. He made contact with her by telegram, and urged her to join him in England, which she was able to do.

The Poles in England had to decide where to settle permanently. With the help of a sponsor in Buffalo, New York, Józef was accepted into the United States.

For a period of time, Józef played his accordion in an orchestra that performed events around Buffalo. At one particular concert he played for a performance of Russian folk dancers, one of whom caught his eye and would become his future wife. Paulina had emigrated from Ukraine to Germany and then to the United States. Jerry and Paulina had four children.

Józef's determination led him to establish a construction company and to eventually build his own house on land he purchased in the hilly and woodsy town of Boston, New York, just south of Buffalo. He was a great father, and the family enjoyed walks in their woods and swimming in their pond. His war stories were exciting, albeit sanitized of any descriptive violence and remarkably modest.

Hardworking, self-reliant, honorable and a great role model, Józef is remembered for his love of family, passion for the study of history, and his great sense of humor. When driving through the German-settled town of Hamburg, New York, if he encountered any modest traffic, he would comment out loud to the confused kids in the backseat, "These Germans! Why can't they ever just stay home?"

When visitors looked with amazement at his lush vegetable gardens, he would explain in a very serious tone, "It's the horse manure... but not just *any* horse manure, I only use *Arabian*."

At family parties, Józef would get out his accordion while chairs and tables were moved aside to free up floor space. Then he would play tangos, waltzes, czardas and mazurkas while everyone danced. His rendition of Ogiński's Polonaise entitled "Farewell to the Homeland" was especially meaningful to him and beloved by family members. Józef loved to celebrate the joys of life and raise a glass in toast with his family and friends, but retained the partisan discipline and never had too much to drink.

Remarkably, he harbored no hatred for German or Russian people. Communists, however, were always held in extreme disdain.

After several years of life in America, as news reached him of Soviet repressions and arrests of his former Polish soldiers, Józef changed his name to Jerome (Jerry) Nurt. He had virtually no contact with his sisters or extended family who remained in Poland, for their safety as well as his own. In 1952, Józef's name and his discovery of the "Secret Order" had become a formal part of the historical record in the United States, during congressional hearings about the Katyń Massacre. The following testimony was provided before a U.S. Congressional Sub-Committee investigating the matter:

Excerpt From

THE UNITED STATES EIGHTY SECOND CONGRESS SECOND SESSION ON INVESTIGATION OF THE MURDER OF THOUSANDS OF POLISH OFFICERS IN THE KATYN FOREST NEAR SMOLENSK, RUSSIA

APRIL 16, 17, 18, and 19, 1952

Testimony of Janusz Prawdzic Szlaski,
of 22 Buer Road, London, S.W.6

Mr. Szalski: (...) I had many opportunities to observe these tactics. When the Russian Armies were virtually destroyed by the Germans in 1941 many of Russian Officers and NKVD officers transferred their allegiance and worked with the German Gestapo, and these officers, especially in the district of Nowogrodek, began then an intensive campaign of collecting the intelligentsia of that area and surrendering it to the Germans. As soon as we discovered this in the Polish underground, we began efforts at destroying this procedure of these Russian NKVD officers selecting the intelligentsia and transferring it to the Germans.

Mr. O'Konski: Why did they transfer the intelligentsia to the Germans?

Mr. Szalski: They wanted to eliminate all the pro-Polish elements in that particular region. After we had succeeded in destroying the intelligence union of the NKVD officers working with the Germans, then those who survived began efforts and contacted us with an effort to try and work with our units against the Germans, We had several conversations their leaders and we did reach an agreement and we did work together and we did manage to destroy many of the installations in various German towns. During this period of cooperation with the remainder of the Russian NKVD with which we were working. We had several conversations to work out various details of points that came up and questions that came up. On December 1, 1943, the Russians invited some of our officers for a series of discussions. After inviting us, we told them to come to one of our underground meeting places, when the Russians got there they attacked us by surprise. They had succeeded in this attack in killing some of our people and capturing others of our people, whom they had taken back to Russia.

Mr. O'Konski: In other words, the Russians asked for a meeting with the leaders of the underground home army?

Mr. Szlaski: Yes.

Mr. O'Konski: And then, when they set the time and place of the meeting with them, the Russians came, and instead of meeting with them, arrested them and killed some of them; is that correct?

Mr. Szlaski: Yes. Those of our people who were away on patrol duty managed to escape this ambush, and then we started a bitter war with the Russian partisans. They frequently attacked our villages and our meeting places.

Mr. O'Konski: That is, the Russians attacked?

Mr. Szlaski: The Russians, and they murdered many of our people, and during one of these battles a Russian Army Staff officer was killed. One of our officers, who searched the body of this staff officer came across a package of papers. This officer is now in the United States.

Mr. O'Konski: What is his name and address, if he knows?

Mr. Szlaski: His name is Józef Niedźwiecki. He lives in Buffalo, and I will give you his exact address a little later. Among the papers that were found on this dead officer was an order in the Russian language issued by the commanding officer of the Russian partisans named Ponomarenko, who until recently was President of White Russia, and is now a member of the Russian politburo.

Mr. O'Konski: In other words, it was a very high ranking Russian officer?

Mr. Szlaski: Yes. The order stated that as of December 1, 1943, all efforts should be made to destroy these Polish underground battalions and to particularly select the officers and noncommissioned officers.

Mr. O'Konski: Ask him if he has a complete copy of that order in his possession.

Mr. Szlaski: I have a copy of that order here which has been translated into the Polish language. The original of this order I have in Poland.

Mr. Flood: Let me see the document. (Document handed to Mr.Flood.) Show this document handed to me by the witness to the stenographer and have it marked as exhibit 31. As I understand it, exhibit 31 the document now marked for identification., is a copy of the order you just described found upon the body of the Russian officer. Is that correct?

Mr. Szalski: Yes.

The last statement of the record was incorrect, in that the Secret Order, Exhibit 31, had been taken from the officer while he was alive. The Secret Order is presented within this work on page 111.

Helena Niedźwiecka also emigrated to America. She married Stanley Filipek, a Polish Army veteran and engineer, and they had three daughters. They also lived for a time in Buffalo before moving to Utica, New York.

She was able to visit Poland, and had some joyous reunions with fellow partisans.

Helena was appreciated for her fantastic cooking, especially many memorable Wigilia meals. She had a cheerful and sunny disposition, a big and frequent smile, and a whistle that could be heard a mile away.

One night in Buffalo she was walking home from work when a mugger grabbed her purse and ran. She had just been paid and had a substantial sum in the purse. She shouted for Stanley, but when he took too long putting on his shoes, Helena remembered her partisan days and ran down the mugger herself, terrified him into dropping the purse, and recovered her hard-earned pay.

She did not tell too many stories about the war. Like so many veterans of World War II, it was usually just too painful and awful to recount in detail. Helena remained close with her brother Józef until the end of his life, and their children and grandchildren grew up together as a tight-knit extended family.

Rufina Niedźwiecka Kwiatkowska stayed in Poland after the war and received a Virtuti Militari medal for her brave actions as a spy, informant and forger during the war. She moved to Gdańsk with her husband and son and lived for many more years under communist government. In later years when Rufina was already past middle age, she was coming home from a meeting of former partisans and her car was pulled over. Rufina was dragged out and beaten by communist party members. She survived this intimidation effort.

ADOLF PILCH emigrated to England and had a successful career as an inventory consultant. He married and had three children. He wrote a memoir entitled *Partyzanci Trzech Puszcz* ("Partisans of Three Forests") describing his war experience. He was active in the Polish Underground Army Ex-Servicemen's Association, and served as president for a time. In 1990, after the fall of communism, he was able to return to Poland and received a much deserved hero's welcome.

ZDZISŁAW NURKIEWICZ stayed in Poland and was hunted down by the new oppressive regime. He worked as a miner under an assumed name, hiding his true identity for years, but was eventually caught and arrested. The communists convicted the innocent and heroic man to a death sentence, but it was commuted to 15 years in prison. He was released after ten years due to poor health.

KACPER MIŁASZEWSKI was sentenced to years in a Soviet gulag but survived and was released in 1948. He married a Polish girl while imprisoned. Fellow prisoners crafted rings out of scrap metal, and a wedding dress from a white sheet. They settled in Wrocław after internment, and had two children.

KAZIMIERZ (CASIMIR) JANKOWSKI also emigrated to the United States and remained friends with Józef Niedźwiecki. "Casey" attended Józef's wedding and was godfather to Józef's son John. He eventually settled in the countryside south of Buffalo, New York, where he lived with his own family.

Research and Sources

Growing up, I knew my father was a war hero. It was common knowledge within our circle of family and friends. He told us stories of the war, often as bedtime stories. He was careful to sanitize them of too much violence. We did not understand the context most of the time.

After he passed away in 1989 we discovered his outlines and writings. They were intriguing. The story of his escape from the SS in Kampinos, the miracle, was written out dramatically and with style. Titled "The Changing Life of a Soldier," it was his first and only completed chapter. The rest of his writing consisted of chronological outlines for the chapters of his memoirs as well as some philosophical writing.

The outlines were mysterious and frustrating. My sister Renata and I tried to figure out what they meant. So began decades of detective work.

I first went to speak with Kazimierz Jankowski, a decorated soldier from my father's own cavalry squadron and my godfather. He had settled in the nearby town of Springville, NY. Casey, as we knew him, spent hours with me discussing his war experience with my father. He helped clarify many outline titles, as well as describing other adventures. He recommended the books *Doliniacy* by Marian Podgóreczny, a soldier from the group, and *Partyzanci Trzech Puszcz*, by Adolf Pilch, for further reading.

Shortly afterward I was able to contact Stanisław Plewako, who runs a website and chat forum about Iwieniec (available at http://www.iwieniec.eu/forum). Mr. Plewako deserves special thanks for his extremely generous time spent helping me with contacts and sources. He was a true gentleman, and helpfully put me in touch with a soldier from my father's squadron: Witold Grzybowski.

Mr. Grzybowski responded to my emails in 2008, and I arranged for my mother to speak to him in Polish. Several more of my father's outline notes were explained to me by Witold directly, and additional clarification was offered through his narration of a TVP Historia documentary entitled "Partyzanci Trzech Puszcz."

I also had conversations with another soldier, Franciszek Kosowicz, by phone. He then wrote me several letters with documents and photos. I got the impression that these great men were happy to help me, and I could tell they had great love and respect for my father.

Stanislaw Plewako's online presence provided great articles on the history of Iwieniec and the Iwieniec Uprising. Also online is a fabulous website from Stanisław Karlik, Kresy24.PL, where I found many articles on the Iwieniec Uprising, on the German occupation, descriptions of Karl Sawinola, aka "The Czech" and more.

I then turned to the monumental task of translating the books most referred to by the soldiers. For this my cousin Danuta Knuth gets many, many thanks. She is a fantastic translator of Polish and was a passionate volunteer because her own mother was Helena Niedźwiecka, my father's sister and an 'Amazon woman' of the partisans. Danuta painstakingly translated *Partyzanci Trzech Puszcz* and *Doliniacy*.

We added *Grupa Kampinos AK*, by Jerzy Koszada, *Z Iwienca i Stolpcow* by Józef Jan Kuźmiński, and *Konspiracja I Powstanie w Kampinosie, 1944*, by Józef Krzyczkowski, for partial translation.

As much work as this was - it took four weeks of Danuta reading and translating while I wrote it out in English, it was a fantastic experience. The books are well-written, often very humorous, and frequent mentions of our own family members brought us goosebumps and tears.

All of the Polish song lyrics throughout the book were translated by Danuta Filipek Knuth, except for *Boże Coś Polskę* (God save Poland), for which I used a translation by the Rev. Thos. Grochowski, C.Ss.R.

The beautiful story of the Mass in the Naliboki forest comes directly from the priest himself, Mieczysław Suwała, in his written account *Boże, coś Polskę' w Puszczy Nalibockiej*.

Over the years I have also read many English language books on Poland in World War II. The most notable ones were:

- Norman Davies, *Rising '44: The Battle for Warsaw* (New York: Penguin Books, 2005).
- Mieczyslaw Klimowicz, *The Last Day of Naliboki: The Untold Story Behind the Massacre* (Baltimore: American Literary Press, 2009).
- Lucjan Krolikowski, *Stolen Childhood: A Saga of Polish War Children*, trans. by Kazmierz J. Rozniatowski (iUniverse, 2001).
- Karolina Lanckorońska, *Michelangelo in Ravensbrück: One Woman's War Against the Nazis* (Da Capo Press, 2007).
- Richard C. Lukas, ed., *Out of the Inferno: Poles Remember the Holocaust* (University Press of Kentucky, 2013).
- Andrzej Micewski, *Cardinal Wyszynski: A Biography* (Bookthrift Co., 1986).
- Roger Moorhouse, *Poland 1939: The Outbreak of World War II* (Basic Books, 2020).
- Wanda E. Pomykalski, *The Horror Trains: A Polish Woman Veteran's Memoir of World War II* by (Minerva Center, 1999).
- Nechama Tec, *In the Lion's Den: The Life of Oswald Rufeisen* (Oxford Univ. Press, 2008).

These all helped lay the groundwork for my overall understanding of what happened in Poland during this period.

It is also worthy to note that unpacking the history of this era is complicated by the fact that Russian partisan accounts often attempted to demonize the Poles to excuse their own murderous behavior. This propaganda is explained in *A Tangled Web: Polish-Jewish Relations in Wartime Northeastern Poland and the Aftermath,* by Mark Paul. This resource is exhaustively researched and dispels many of the falsehoods and slanders directed at the Polish Home Army by Soviet-affiliated sources.

Here is one example of Józef Niedźwiecki's outlines.

1. Efforts to escape Nazi onslaught
2. Long and dangerous retreat, bombing and strafing. Lancut and hand gun.
3. Pistol transfer and first encounter with Red Army
4. Arrest and forced transition into Russia.
5. Jump to freedom and hiding
6. Soviet occupation and Sovietization.
7. First attempts of conspiracy. Fire drills
8. Soviet Secret Police on a trail through infiltration
9. Arms hide outs and betrayal. List of secret membership
10. Soviet mentality understood. Precautions always taken.
11. Betrayal and a trap on a road.
12. Capture and delivery into NKVD prison Minsk.
13. Continuous interrogation, usually at night 3 or 4 AM till morning. Subtle psychology and beating not difficult to figure out what they are after

JOHN ROMAN NURT

Here is a portion of the chapter regarding the escape from the SS in Kampinos, as my father wrote it.

THE CHANGING LUCK OF A SOLDIER.
(From the notebook of a Guerrilla fighter.)

It was almost a daybreak and the visibility increased every minute. I was riding at the head of the column which consisted of the 1st and 2nd platoons of my cavalry squadron. The 3rd platoon was on a reconessanse and some distance ahead of us. We were on the move for two consecutive nights since we left our forest bases.

The Warsaw uprising just ended, survivors capitulated. Since that time the Luftwaffe and strong enemy-ground units increased pressure upon remaining areas of resistance and particularly upon our group. We knew we could not last there much longer and decided to move to safer grounds. To accomplish this we moved by night when Germans seldom interfered.

As we rode along I signalled platoon leaders to join me. We had to stop for rest. Courier was dispatched to halt 3rd platoon, too. As soon as the men dismounted they started to look for some dry spot on the ground and after a while most of them were fast asleep.

I remember I was not feeling sleepy at all. Our general situation was far from rosy. Germans were using major units to pacify the countryside. Yet the Russian front was less than 50. miles away. Since the Warsaw eruption it became strangely quiet and the Nazis enjoyed a free hand in their wicked designs against us. For some time now we suspected Stalin wanted and gave tacid consent to our destruction. The irony of all this was that the end of the Third Reich seemed almost in sight. Our long struggle and five years of Nazi occupation nearly over.

My thoughts were abruptly interupted by two fast approaching figures. They were boys from the 3rd platoon with the message. "Enemy patrol heading this way. "Their platoon leader suggested he would let the Germans through.

I promptly ordered the 1st platoon to form a semi-circle on the edge of the woods, 2nd platoon to provide cover with its machine guns. And soon we were watching unaware Germans walking straight into the trap. When they got close enough I gave the signal to close in. It was a complete surprise. As soon as they noticed us they stopped and stared with horror all around them. Where they looked they could see our troop closing in

Appendix

Notes by Chapter

Note from the editors: John Nurt passed away from terminal cancer before this appendix could be completed. Much of this work was done while the author was in the hospital and at home in the weeks leading up to his passing, while the rest was completed posthumously. Due to the unusual circumstances, this is a good-faith effort at documenting cited works and reference materials, but there may be unintentional mistakes. Corrections from historians are welcome, and will be taken into account for future editions.

Chapter 1: Lwów

The events in this chapter are drawn from Józef's notes and outlines, as well as conversations with the author. For more general descriptions of the Battle of Lwów and events leading to it, see:

- Bartłomiej Kozłowski, "'Wybory' do Zgromadzeń Ludowych Zachodniej Ukrainy i Zachodniej Białorusi" archived via the 'Wayback Machine' on 6/28/2006 at https://web.archive.org/web/20060628125314/http://wiadomosci.polska.pl/kalendarz/kalendarium/article.htm?id=132394. (trans. from Polish).

- Artur Leinwand, "Defense of Lwów in 1939," *Lwow.com*, at https://www.lwow.com.pl/rocznik/obrona39.html (Instytut Lwowski, 1991) (trans. from Polish).

- Roger Moorhouse, *First To Fight: The Polish War 1939* (Bodley Head, 2019), p. 205-219.

- Steven Zaloga, *Poland 1939: The Birth of Blitzkrieg* (Oxford: Osprey Publishing Ltd., 2002).

Chapter 2: First escape

Józef's notes document the train escape, and the story was told many times to family and friends. Józef's verbal story of his "leap to freedom" is best recollected by Richard Nurt from Józef's description. It is unclear how many Polish prisoners escaped with Józef; it is believed that the number was somewhere between 5 and 9. Also, it is not known what type of train he was on: the description of the train itself is artistic license.

The Katyn Forest massacre is well documented. For additional reading see:

- Anna M. Cienciala, et al, eds., *Katyn: A Crime Without Punishment. Annals of Communism Series* (Yale University Press, 2008).

- Norman Davies, *No Simple Victory: World War II in Europe, 1939–1945* (Viking Books, 2007), p. 6-7; 13-14; 312.

- "The History of Katyn Massacre," *Mieroszewski Centre*, 2022, at https://katynpromemoria.pl/the-history-of-katyn-massacre/?lang=en.

- "Katyn Timeline," *Kresy Family Polish WWII History Group*, at https://www.kresyfamily.com/3-katyn-timeline.html.

- Richard C. Lukas, *Forgotten Holocaust: The Poles under German Occupation 1939-1944* (Hippocrene Books, 1997).

- Katarczyna Utracka, "The Katyn Massacre–Mechanisms of Genocide", *The Warsaw Institute Review*, 18 May 2020, at https://warsawinstitute.review/issue-2020/the-katyn-massacre-mechanisms-of-genocide/.

- Tadeusz Wolsza, "The Katyn Massacre, its Chronology, Scale, Victims, and Unpunished Perpetrators," *Polish History Museum in Warsaw* at https://polishhistory.pl/the-katyn-massacre-its-chronology-scale-victims-and-unpunished-perpetrators/.

Chapter 3: Soviet Occupation

The description of Iwieniec derives from numerous sources, most notably from:

- Mieczysław Suwała, "'Boże, coś Polskę' w Puszczy Nalibockiej," in Julian Humeński, ed., Udział kapelanów wojskowych w drugiej wojnie światowej (Warsaw: Akademia Teologii Katolickiej, 1984).

The story of the childhood 'Olympics' was told to the author by Józef.

NKVD attempts to eliminate Polish opposition through arrests and deportation were described by Józef to the author, but are well documented in numerous sources, including:

- Marek Jan Chodakiewicz, *Between Nazis and Soviets: Occupation Politics in Poland, 1939-1947* (Lexington Books: 2004).

- Richard C. Lukas, *Forgotten Holocaust: The Poles under German Occupation 1939-1944*, 3rd ed. (Hippocrene Books, 2001).

- Timothy Snyder, *Bloodlands: Europe between Hitler and Stalin* (New York: Basic Books, 2010).

Parts of the story of the formation of the Polish Underground, such as Józef's instruction to Helena regarding the importance of secrecy, were told to the author. For additional details, such as early meetings being conducted at the Niedźwiecki household, see:

- Marian Podgóreczny, *Doliniacy* (Warsaw: Mireki, 2013).

The story about Jan dancing with the broom was often told by Józef to friends and family. It is not clear if this anecdote happened precisely at this point in the chronology, but represents the author's best guess combined with artistic license.

Józef and Jan's leadership positions are well documented in numerous locations. See:

- Witold Grzybowski, *Spis żołnierzy Zgrupowania Stołpecko-Nalibockiego Armii Krajowej* (Warsaw: Witold Grzybowski, 2014). Accessible at http://iwieniec.eu/AK/index.html.

- Stanisław Karlik, "Partyzanci z Puszczy Nalibockiej 1939–44," *Kresy24.pl*, at https://kresy24.pl/partyzanci-z-puszczy-nalibockiej-1939-44/ (trans. from Polish).

- Kazimierz Krajewski, *Na Ziemia Nowogródek 'NÓW': Nowogródek District of the Home Army* (Warsaw: Pax, 1997).

- Józef Jan Kuźmiński, *Z Iwienca i Stolpcow* (Mireki, 2014).

- Marian Podgóreczny, *Doliniacy* (Warsaw: Mireki, 2013).

The discussion of Szabunia, the spy, and conditions in Iwienec under the NKVD are mainly drawn from Józef's notes and verbal stories, and:

- Mieczyslaw Klimowicz, *The Last Day of Naliboki: The Untold Story Behind the Massacre* (Baltimore: American Literary Press, 2009), p. 112-126.

The NKVD arrests are well documented, but the specific details regarding the typical methods of nighttime visits etc. derive from the author's interviews with Dr. Walter Orlowski, conducted over several years, circa 2017-2019. In his childhood, Orlowski was deported from Poland by the NKVD and sent with his family to a Soviet gulag.

Chapter 4: Capture and Prison

The information about Józef and Jan's capture and imprisonment by the NKVD is based on various family accounts, originally conveyed by Józef and Helena Niedzwiecka Filipek. There is some confusion on the dates that this period covers. In the book they are described as being captured in the autumn of 1940, but this is a conservative guess. Józef's outlines suggest that he and Jan were in prison for fourteen months, from April 1940 to June 22nd, 1941 (the date the death march commenced), and both Helena and Józef spoke of the imprisonment as lasting fourteen months. The NKVD records have different dates however.

The NKVD arrest records of Josef and Jan are available via the Instytut Pamieci Narodowej's 'Indeks Represjonowanychi' as follows:

- Józef: https://indeksrepresjonowanych.pl/indeksrepresjonowanych/pl/szczegoly1.jsp?id=243710

- Jan: https://indeksrepresjonowanych.pl/indeksrepresjonowanych/pl/szczegoly1.jsp?id=243709

Nazwisko: **Niedźwiecki**
Imię: **Józef**
Drugie Imię:
Imię ojca: **Franciszek**
Imię matki:
Data urodzenia: **1916**

LP	Opis losów	Początek r	m	d	Koniec r	m	d	Kraj	Woj/Oblast	Pow.	Miej.
1	Areszt	1940	11	22							
2	Wyrok	1941	5	28							
3	Łagier										Siewwostłag
4	Zwolnienie	1941	6								

LP	opis źródła	sygnatura
1.	Karta ewidencyjna w kartotece osób podlegających rehabilitacji (Archiwum KGB Republiki Białoruś w Mińsku) - numer karty	KMi- -31022
2.	Teczka personalna osoby aresztowanej przechowywana w Archiwum KGB RB w Mińsku	TMi- -28767-S
3.	Wykaz spraw prowadzonych przez organa NKWD Zachodniej Ukrainy i Białorusi (wybór z Księgi Rejestracji Spraw Archiwalno-Śledczych NKWD ZSRR), kopia Ośrodek KARTA - tom, strona, pozycja (numer nadany w OK).	ZUB- -365-166-19

Nazwisko: **Niedźwiecki**
Imię: **Jan**
Drugie Imię:
Imię ojca: **Franciszek**
Imię matki:
Data urodzenia: **1913**

LP	Opis losów	Początek r	m	d	Koniec r	m	d	Kraj	Woj/Oblast	Pow.	Miej.
1	Areszt	1940	11	22							
2	Wyrok	1941	5	28							
3	Łagier										Siewwostłag
4	Zwolnienie	1941	6								

LP	opis źródła	sygnatura
1.	Karta ewidencyjna w kartotece osób podlegających rehabilitacji (Archiwum KGB Republiki Białoruś w Mińsku) - numer karty	KMi- -31021
2.	Teczka personalna osoby aresztowanej przechowywana w Archiwum KGB RB w Mińsku	TMi- -28767-S
3.	Wykaz spraw prowadzonych przez organa NKWD Zachodniej Ukrainy i Białorusi (wybór z Księgi Rejestracji Spraw Archiwalno-Śledczych NKWD ZSRR), kopia Ośrodek KARTA - tom, strona, pozycja (numer nadany w OK).	ZUB- -365-166-20

The chronology of Józef's transport between NKVD prisons, ending in Minsk, comes from Józef's notes as does the description of what happened in the NKVD prison. However, the true names of the Russian jailers and interrogators are unknown and have been fictionalized for purposes of readability.

The story regarding the Polish prisoners teasing the Russian guards about the Soviets' ability to grow food was told to the author by one of the partisans that was interviewed for this work. The editors could not identify which of them passed it along this specific vignette. While not documentable, it is at minimum representative of how the Polish prisoners attempted to fight back in small ways against their captors.

Chapter 5: German Attack - Death March

Mainly sourced from Józef's notes and verbal descriptions.

The NKVD prison massacres of 1941 and horrors of the death marches are well documented online. For more reading on the NKVD prisons and prisoner massacres, see:

- "'Chronicles of Terror' testimony database," *Witold Pilecki Institute of Solidarity and Valor*, at https://instytutpileckiego.pl/en/kolekcje-cyfrowe/zapisy-terroru.

- "Deportation," *Kresy Family Polish History Group* at https://www.kresyfamily.com/3-deportation.html.

- Jennifer Popowycz, "The 1941 NKVD Prison Massacres in Western Ukraine," *The National WWII Museum*, 7 June 2021, at https://www.nationalww2museum.org/war/articles/1941-nkvd-prison-massacres-western-ukraine.

For additional reading on the 'Operation Barbarossa' German attack on Russia on June 22nd, which caused the emptying of the NKVD prison and commencement of the death march, see:

- Tadeusz Piotrowski, *Poland's Holocaust: Ethnic Strife, Collaboration with Occupying Forces and Genocide in the Second Republic, 1918-1947* (Jefferson, NC: McFarland & Co., 2007).

- Marian Podgóreczny, *Doliniacy* (Warsaw: Mireki, 2013).

- Timothy Snyder, *Bloodlands: Europe Between Hitler and Stalin* (Basic Books, 2010).

- Joanna Stankiewicz-Januszczak, *Marsz śmierci. Ewakuacja więźniów z Mińska do Czerwieni 24–27 czerwca 1941* (Warsaw: Oficyna Wydawnicza Volumen i Rada Ochrony Pamięci Walk i Męczeństwa, 1999).

The remaining prisoners' arrival at the third NKVD prison, and description of German bombing that freed Józef and Jan, was described by Józef to Michael Romanych (husband of Helena's daughter Alice) during a conversation about the war circa May of 1975.

Chapter 6: Another Journey Home

Post-escape travel back to Iwieniec from Józef's and Helena's descriptions. Józef described this experience to the author and various family members, including specifics such as foraging in gardens and eating crayfish. The stories that Jan and Józef recount to each other on this walk are real stories well known in the family. It is not known that this conversation occurred during this travel. The author includes them here under artistic license in order to illustrate the brothers' personalities.

The spotting of Józef and Jan returning to Iwieniec by a nephew derives from numerous family accounts, and was recorded in November 1994 in an interview with Helena Niedzwiecka Filipek conducted by Larissa Niedzwiecka Doyle.

Story regarding Biały, who betrayed Jan and Józef, begging for and receiving mercy was told to several family members by Józef and confirmed by Helena.

Chapter 7: Conspiracy

The attempts by Polish partisans to help Jewish neighbors from Nazi persecution are well documented. For instance, partisan Henryk Werakso recounts efforts in the Spring of 1942 to save Jews in the Stolpce ghetto from a planned liquidation. In one instance, Werakso hid three Jewish women in a wagon which he was purporting to use to carry bags from a lime pit, eventually succeeding despite a tense encounter with a German sergeant. For more on this story, see:

- Richard C. Lukas, ed., *Out of the Inferno: Poles Remember the Holocaust*, 175-177 (Lexington, KY: The University Press of Kentucky, 1989).

Karl ("Czech", "Sawinola") Cavill's pet jest about his mood depending on how recently he had committed murder:

- Józef Jan Kuźmiński, *Z Iwienca i Stolpcow* (Warsaw: Mireki, 2014), p. 41.
- Marian Podgóreczny, *Doliniacy* (Warsaw: Mireki, 2013), p. 46.

Description of the development of the underground in 1942 under Kaspar Miłaszewski:

- Marian Podgóreczny, *Doliniacy* (Warsaw: Mireki, 2013), p. 58-60.

Info about Kacpar Miłaszewski:

- "Bohater Powstania Iwenieckiego por. Kasper Miłaszewski pochowany we Wrocławiu," *Armia Krajowa Zgorzelec*, at https://armiakrajowazgorzelec.blogspot.com/2016/11/bohater-powstania-iwenieckiego-por.html (trans. from Polish).
- Stanisław Karlik, "Partyzanci z Puszczy Nalibockiej 1939-44," *Kresy24.pl*, at https://kresy24.pl/partyzanci-z-puszczy-nalibockiej-1939-44/ (trans. from Polish).
- Paweł Kosowicz, "W Puszczy Nalibockiej," *Tygodnik Powszechny*, no. 40, 1978, available at http://www.iwieniec.eu/AK/Tyg%20Powsz_Iwieniec.htm (trans. from Polish).
- Kazimierz Krajewski, *Na straconych posterunkach* (Wydawnictwo Literackie, 2015).
- Adolph Pilch, *Partyzanci Trzech Puszcz* (Mireki, 2013).
- Marian Podgóreczny, *Doliniacy* (Warsaw: Mireki, 2013).
- Marian Podgóreczny, *Zgrupowanie Stołpeckie-Nalibockie Armii Krajowej: Oszczerstwa i fakty. Wywiad z dowódcą Zgrupowania, cichociemnym, mjr Adolfem Pilchem ps. „Góra", „Dolina,"* (Sopot: Iwieniec.eu, 2010).

On choosing *noms de guerre*:

- Jerzy Koszada, *Grupa Kampinos: Partyzanckie zgrupowanie Armii Krajowej* (Warsaw: ZP GRUPA, 2007).

Story regarding Jan's new horse. Józef recounted the name Jan gave to the horse, and it is clear that the partisans routinely used the Kul estate for provisions and as a training location. For more on the Kul estate, see generally:

- Stanisław Karlik, "Partyzanci z Puszczy Nalibockiej 1939–44," *Kresy24.pl*, at https://kresy24.pl/partyzanci-z-puszczy-nalibockiej-1939-44/ (trans. from Polish).

- Stanisław Karlik, "Powstanie Iwienieckie 19 czerwca 1943"," *Kresy24.pl*, at https://kresy24.pl/powstanie-iwienieckie-19-czerwca-1943%E2%80%B3-1/ (trans. from Polish).

- Marian Podgóreczny, *Doliniacy* (Warsaw: Mireki, 2013).

The conversation about the horse represents the author's interpretation of the likely dialogue based upon Józef's descriptions.

The Underground's placement of agents in key roles, such as Rufina's job in Karl Cavill's office, is well documented in many sources. For a photo with caption describing Rufina's role with the German military police, see:

- Stanisław Karlik, "Polska konspiracja w Iwieńcu w latach 1939-43," *Kresy24.pl*, at https://kresy24.pl/polska-konspiracja-w-iwiencu-w-latach-1939-43/ (trans. from Polish).

Rufina's role in particular was described to the author by Renata Bork, granddaughter of Rufina. Polish journalist Stanislaw Karlik indicated to the author that in one instance a woman in Cavill's office warned Karlik's uncle, who had been ordered to report to Cavill's command, that he was in danger–thus potentially saving his life. It is believed that this woman would likely have been Rufina.

The description of the tenuous working relationship between the Polish and Russian partisans, and events that occurred when the Russians breached that relationship, is well documented. See e.g.:

- Mieczyslaw Klimowicz, *The Last Day of Naliboki: The Untold Story Behind the Massacre* (Baltimore: American Literary Press, 2009).

- Longin Kołosowski & Witold Grzybowski, "Zgrupowanie Stołpecko – Nalibockie AK," *Iwieniec.eu*, 2007, at http://www.iwieniec.eu/AK/Iwieniecka%20AK.pdf.

- Mark Paul, *A Tangled Web: Polish-Jewish Relations in Wartime Northeastern Poland and the Aftermath*, (Toronto: PEFINA Press, 2016), available for download at http://kpk-toronto.org/wp-content/uploads/obrona_mark_paul_2010_tangled_web1.pdf.

- Marian Podgóreczny, *Doliniacy* (Warsaw: Mireki, 2013), p. 18.

The scene depicting Jan and Józef witnessing the execution of Jan's friend is based on Józef's account as told to John Nurt and Richard Nurt. Richard specifically recalls Józef recounting this to him around 1980. The dialog is artistic license but the rest of the scene is as Józef described it. The location of the scene is a best guess, based on the fact that the Orthodox cemetery was a known execution area used by Cavill, as documented in sources such as:

- Mieczyslaw Klimowicz, *The Last Day of Naliboki: The Untold Story Behind the Massacre* (Baltimore: American Literary Press, 2009)

- Longin Kołosowski & Witold Grzybowski, "Zgrupowanie Stołpecko – Nalibockie AK," *Iwieniec.eu*, 2007, at http://www.iwieniec.eu/AK/Iwieniecka%20AK.pdf.

- Marian Podgóreczny, *Doliniacy*, (Warsaw: Mireki, 2013)

The German "registration" of young men in Iwieniec on June 19, 1943, and events leading to the uprising is a seminal event in the history of the Polish Underground, and is described in a great many works. See e.g. Podgóreczny's *Doliniacy* at pp. 62-70.

Jozef and Jan involved in the planning of the Uprising can be found in several sources, including:

- Stanislaw Karlik, "Powstanie Iwienieckie – 19 czerwca 1943 r.," *IV Rozbior Polski,* at https://www.ivrozbiorpolski.pl/index.php?page=powstanie-iwienieckie (trans. from Polish).

Drawing of match sticks:

- Paweł Kosowicz, "W Puszczy Nalibockiej," *Tygodnik Powszechny*, no. 40, 1978, available at http://www.iwieniec.eu/AK/Tyg%20Powsz_Iwieniec.htm (trans. from Polish).

- Józef Jan Kuźmiński, *Z Iwieńca i Stołpców* (Mireki, 2014)

- Marian Podgóreczny, *Doliniacy* (Warsaw: Mireki, 2013)

The dialog between Jan and Józef about Jan's role in the Uprising is artistic license, but it is known from Józef, Helena and other sources that Józef tried to convince Jan to switch roles with him, and that he had a strong sense of foreboding about Jan taking this job.

The oath taking place in the Niedźwiecki home is documented in several places, including:

- Paweł Kosowicz, "W Puszczy Nalibockiej," *Tygodnik Powszechny*, no. 40, 1978, available at http://www.iwieniec.eu/AK/Tyg%20Powsz_Iwieniec.htm (trans. from Polish).

- Marian Podgóreczny, *Doliniacy*, (Warsaw: Mireki, 2013)

Chapter 8: The Iwieniec Uprising

Józef's tasks during the Uprising are per his notes and recollections. Podgóreczny's *Doliniacy* is also helpful in this regard.

It is not known for sure who fired the shot eliminating the German observer in the 'stork's nest' atop the roof of the gendarmerie building. According to one source, it was partisan Michał Romanowski who commenced the raid with this markmanship. In a competing account, partisan Wacław Nowicki attests that it was Jan Niedzwieki who fired the shot. Nowicki's account is documented in Stanislaw Karlik's article entitled "Powstanie Iwienieckie – 19 czerwca 1943 r.," available at https://www.ivrozbiorpolski.pl/index.php?page=powstanie-iwienieckie. While the author chose to attribute the shot to Jan Niedwiecki based on his research and interviews with other partisans, he did feel it important to acknowledge that the record is not clear.

Additional sources for the Iwieniec Uprising include:

- Stanisław Karlik, "Powstańcy iwienieccy," *Kresy24.pl*, 2013, at https://kresy24.pl/powstancy-iwieniecky/ (trans. from Polish).

- Stanisław Karlik, "'Powstania Iwienieckiego 19.06.1943 r.," *Kresy24.pl*, at https://kresy24.pl/bilans-powstania-iwienieckiego/ (trans. from Polish).

- Karlik, "Powstanie Iwienieckie – 19 czerwca 1943 r.", *IV Rozbior Polski*, at https://www.ivrozbiorpolski.pl/index.php?page=powstanie-iwienieckie (trans. from Polish).

- Yvonne Kasta, "Iwieniecka konspiracja i zbrojne powstanie," *Kresy24.pl*, at https://kresy24.pl/iwonna-kasta-iwieniecka-konspiracja-i-zbrojne-powstanie/ (trans. from Polish).

- Paweł Kosowicz, "W Puszczy Nalibockiej," *Tygodnik Powszechny*, no. 40, 1978, available at http://www.iwieniec.eu/AK/Tyg%20Powsz_Iwieniec.htm (trans. from Polish).

- Kazimierz Krajewski, "Powstanie iwienieckie i zapomniane boje w Puszczy Nalibockiej," *Biuletyn Informacyjny AK* (May, 2013).

- Józef Jan Kuźmiński, *Z Iwieńca i Stołpców* (Mireki, 2014).

- Adolph Pilch, *Partyzanci Trzech Puszcz* (Mireki, 2013).

- Marian Podgóreczny, *Doliniacy* (Warsaw: Mireki, 2013), p. 42-74.

- Marian Podgóreczny, *Zgrupowanie Stołpeckie–Nalibockie Armii Krajowej: Oszczerstwa i fakty. Wywiad z dowódcą Zgrupowania, cichociemnym, mjr Adolfem Pilchem ps. „Góra", „Dolina,"* (Sopot: Iwieniec.eu, 2010).

- Mieczysław Suwała, "'Boże, coś Polskę' w Puszczy Nalibockiej," in Julian Humeński, ed., *Udział kapelanów wojskowych w drugiej wojnie światowej* (Warsaw: Akademia Teologii Katolickiej, 1984).

- Piotr Zawada, "Powstanie Iwienieckie 1943 r.," *Szwadron Kawalerii*, at https://kawaleriaochotnicza.pl/2019/07/09/powstanie-iwienieckie-1943-r/ (trans. from Polish).

The story about "Czech" (Cavill) hiding in the sawmill is recounted in:

- Adolph Pilch, *Partyzanci Trzech Puszcz*, 2013 ed. (Mireki, 2013)

The scene with Józef's grief after the death of Jan, his return home and conversations with family members is artistic license based on family recollections.

Józef's vow to kill "Czech" was described to the author by Józef, Helena and Józef's wife Paulina.

The execution of the Franciscans at the monastery is documented in:

- Stanisław Karlik, "Bilans Powstania Iwienieckiego 19.06.1943 r.," *Kresy24.pl*, at https://kresy24.pl/bilans-powstania-iwienieckiego/ (trans. from Polish).

The story about "Czech" tormenting the family at the dinner table before executing them was told to Richard Nurt and others by Józef.

General Ponomarenko's secret directive against the Polish partisans:

- Bogdan Musiał, "Memorandum Pantelejmona Ponomarienki z 20 stycznia 1943 r.: 'O zachowaniu się Polaków i niektórych naszych zadaniach,'" *Pamięć i Sprawiedliwość* 1, no. 9 (2006): 379-385 (Instytut Pamięci Narodowcj, 2006)

- Mark Paul, *A Tangled Web: Polish-Jewish Relations in Wartime Northeastern Poland and the Aftermath* (Toronto: PEFINA Press, 2016).

- Tadeusz Piotrowski, *Poland's Holocaust* (McFarland & Company, 1998), p. 98-99.

- Marian Podgóreczny, *Doliniacy* (Warsaw: Mireki, 2013)

The lyrics to "Za Niemen" are translated here by Danuta Filipek Knuth.

Chapter 9: Naliboki Forest - Operation Hermann

Jan Jakubowski and Józef Niedźwiecki singled out for leadership:

- Marian Podgóreczny, *Doliniacy* (Warsaw: Mireki, 2013)

Sources for "Operation Hermann" include:

- Marek Jan Chodakiewicz, *Between Nazis and Soviets: Occupation Politics in Poland, 1939-1947* (Lexington Books).

- Witold Grzybowski, *Spis żołnierzy Zgrupowania Stołpecko-Nalibockiego Armii Krajowej* (Warsaw: Witold Grzybowski, 2014).

- Kazimierz Krajewski, "Powstanie iwienieckie i zapomniane boje w Puszczy Nalibockiej," *Biuletyn Informacyjny AK* (May, 2013).

- Józef Jan Kuźmiński, *Z Iwieńca i Stołpców* (Mireki, 2014).

- Richard C. Lukas, *Forgotten Holocaust: The Poles under German Occupation 1939-1944* (Hippocrene Books, 1997).

- Adolph Pilch, *Partyzanci Trzech Puszcz*, 2013 ed. (Mireki, 2013)

- Marian Podgóreczny, *Doliniacy* (Warsaw: Mireki, 2013)

- Timothy Snyder, *Bloodlands: Europe between Hitler and Stalin* (New York: Basic Books, 2010).

Additional details in this chapter are from Józef's descriptions.

The scene of the attack on the grassy dike in the swamp is mainly drawn from:

- Józef Jan Kuźmiński, *Z Iwieńca i Stołpców* (Mireki, 2014)

More information about the SS Dirlewanger Brigade can be found in these sources:

- "36th Waffen Grenadier Division of the SS," *Fandom.com*, at https://military-history.fandom.com/wiki/36th_Waffen_Grenadier_Division_of_the_SS.

- Matthew Gault, "The Awful History of Real Life 'Suicide Squads': The Vile Story of the Nazis' 'Dirlewanger Brigade,'" Medium.com, at https://medium.com/war-is-boring/the-vile-story-of-the-nazis-dirlewanger-brigade-8a7da5dedoc7.

- Cezary Gmyz, "Dirlewanger, czyli bestia," *Rzeczpospolita* (29 Dec. 2008), at https://www.rp.pl/historia/art15866981-dirlewanger-czyli-bestia (trans. from Polish).

- Christian Ingrao, *The SS Dirlewanger Brigade: The History of the Black Hunters*, (New York: Skyhorse Pub., 2011).

- Włodzimierz Nowak & Angelika Kuźniak, "My Warsaw Madness: The Other Side of the Warsaw Uprising," *Gazeta Wyborcza* (27 Aug. 2004) at http://www.warsawuprising.com/witness/schenk.htm.

- Timothy Snyder, *Bloodlands: Europe between Hitler and Stalin* (New York: Basic Books, 2010) pp. 241–242, 246, 304.

The aftermath of the swamp attack also draws on details from Podgóreczny's *Doliniacy*.

Helena Niedzwiecka Filipek recounted the story about hiding under the blanket of moss to the author while traveling from Buffalo to Barneveld, New York in 1977. The identity of her cohort in hiding is not known for sure, but it may have been Ewa Hrynkiewicz or Wanda Mikucka.

'Bohun' was the pseudonym of Alexander Koziol and it is believed that he was the soldier who led Józef to Helena, but this is not known for sure.

Information about 'Bohun' and other Kampinos group soldiers who died in 1944 can be found at:

- Jerzy Koszada, "Wykaz żołnierzy Ppwstania Warszawskiego walczących w 'Grupie Kampinos,'" *Historical Committee of the Environment "Kampinos Group" of the World Association of Home Army Soldiers*, at https://ak-obroza-kampinos.waw.pl/411.html (trans. from Polish).

The rest of the chapter is based on Józef's stories as recalled by John and Richard Nurt, as well as the previously mentioned sources on Operation Hermann.

Chapter 10: Rebuilding

All dialogue from the scene of Józef's meeting with Miłaszewski and Pilch is artistic license, but is based on known facts. Partisans that fought with Józef, such as Kazmierz Jankowski, Witold Grzybowski and Francisek Kosowicz told the author in interviews and correspondence about their love and respect for Józef and the loyalty of his platoon members.

The goal to establish a counterforce to the Russian partisans:

- Mark Paul, *A Tangled Web: Polish-Jewish Relations in Wartime Northeastern Poland and the Aftermath* (Toronto: PEFINA Press, 2016).

The Mass in the woods description is from:

- Mieczysław Suwała, "'Boże, coś Polskę' w Puszczy Nalibockiej," in Julian Humeński, ed., *Udział kapelanów wojskowych w drugiej wojnie światowej* (Warsaw: Akademia Teologii Katolickiej, 1984).

The rest of the chapter details are mainly drawn from Józef's stories and notes, Podgóreczny's *Doliniacy*, and:

- Adolph Pilch, *Partyzanci Trzech Puszcz*, 2013 ed. (Mireki, 2013)

"Anthem of the Home Army" and "White Roses" lyrics translated by Danuta Filipek Knuth.

"God save Poland" lyrics translation of the Rev. Thos. Grochowski, C.Ss.R, in the public domain.

Chapter 11: Medic

Drawn from Kuźmiński's *Z Iwiencu i Stolpcow*. The scene of Józef's conversation with Kuźmiński regarding the medic's injured feet is based on Kuźmiński's description. The original Polish text in Kuzminski's own words reads:

> "W drugiej połowie stycznia - a był już wieczór do naszego mieszkania weszli nasi żołnierze na czele z Józkiem Niedźwiedzkim kpr. z 78 pp WP, który był w Puszczy Nalibockiej żołnierzem kawalerii. Zdziwił się, że żyjemy, bo dowództwo nowo sformowanego oddziału zaliczyło nas w straty. Chciał nas zabrać ze sobą. Oddział kwaterował pod Iwieńcem. Nie było żadnej opieki sanitarnej. Powiedziałem mu o opinii chirurga. Powiedział, bym się stąd nigdzie nie ruszał - 'bo wiesz, z nami żartów nie ma.'"

Chapter 12: Soviet Storm Clouds

This chapter is based on information from the books *Doliniaci*, by Podgóreczny, Pilch's *Partyzanci Trzech Puszcz*, Paul's *A Tangled Web*, and Józef's notes and stories.

The meeting with the Frunze Brigade is sourced from Józef's notes and stories.

Józef's notes mention the officers lecturing the AK partisans about strict moral discipline, and how important this was.

Chapter 13: First Injury

This chapter is from Józef's description. His three injuries are documented in official military forms. Józef's philosophical thoughts are based on various writings of his.

The doctor's instruction to play the accordion as therapy for his injury was a story often recounted by Józef, and also his wife Paulina.

Paulina is the source of the story about Józef practicing with a pistol in hopes of killing Czech.

Chapter 14: The Saving of Walma

Józef's description and notes. Unfortunately, more documentation is lacking. This event is based on a combination of Józef's stories about a rescue mission riding Bucephalus (although it is not known whether that was related to "Walma" specifically), and a vague note in Jozef's timeline about "My Saving of Walma." The author did his best to piece together where in the chronology this would have fit. The story is recollected by John and Richard Nurt.

Chapter 15: The Deluge

Dubov and Wasilewsky's visit to the Polish camp is from Pilch's book *Partyzanci Trzech Puszcz*, as well as the following details about Pelka and Nurkiewicz, and Warakomski's speech.

The Soviet propaganda assault is drawn from Podgóreczny's *Doliniaci* and Paul's *A Tangled Web*.

The section on Dubov's invitation to Pelka and the war council is drawn from the books *Partyzanci Trzech Puszcz*, by Pilch, Podgóreczny's *Doliniaci*, and:

- Marian Podgóreczny, "Ryszard Lewin, ps. 'Luźny' nie żyje," *Kresy24.pl* at https://kresy24.pl/ryszard-lewin-ps-luzny-nie-zyje/ (trans. from Polish).

The execution of the Russian Frolow, the two brothers, and the other details from Brodek are described in Mark Paul's *A Tangled Web*.

The capture of the large group of Soviet partisans, and the next several paragraphs are drawn from Pilch's *Partyzanci Trzech Puszcz* and Józef's notes.

The finding of corpses in the melting snow is a detail from Paul's *A Tangled Web*.

The half-dead appearance of Pilch and his men, and most of the details in the rest of the chapter can be found in Pilch's *Partyzanci Trzech Puszcz* and Podgóreczny's *Doliniaci*.

The ceasefire agreement, and the events leading up to it are documented in many places, in particular Pilch's *Partyzanci Trzech Puszcz* and Podgóreczny's *Doliniaci*. They are also mentioned in the accounts of partisans Longin Kołosowski and Witold Grzybowski:

- Longin Kołosowski & Witold Grzybowski, "Zgrupowanie Stołpecko – Nalibockie AK," (Iwieniec.eu, 2007), at http://www.iwieniec.eu/AK/Iwieniecka%20AK.pdf.

Chapter 16: The Secret Order

The first few paragraphs are based on Józef's descriptions. The capture of the secret order is documented in many places, most notably in US Congressional testimony, 1952.

The fact that the commissar and his wife were shot by the NKVD is from Podgóreczny's *Doliniacy* as well as multiple other sources.

Pilch's book *Partyzanci Trzech Puszcz* is an additional source for the events of this chapter.

It wasn't until after the war that another original copy of this Soviet order was discovered. Copy no. 9, was found in the National Archives of the Republic of Belarus, in Minsk. Józef's is copy no. 7.

Chapter 17: Ski Adventure

From Józef's notes and his stories about the ski adventure, as recollected by Richard and John Nurt.

It is not known exactly how many men accompanied Józef on this mission, but it was likely a small group.

The scene with the introduction of Jozef's new nickname "Avalanche" is artistic license. It is known that he acquired that nickname through his men, but not exactly when or where. This dialogue is invented for narrative purposes.

Chapter 18: Fighting the Soviets

Most of the information in this chapter is drawn from Pilch's *Partyzanci Trzech Puszcz* and Podgóreczny's *Doliniaci*.

Additional sources on the battle in Kamien:

- Longin Kołosowski's interview from the "Oral History Archive", *Muzeum Powstania Warszawskiego*, at https://www.1944.pl/archiwum-historii-mowionej/longin-kolosowski,745.html (trans. from Polish).

- Kazimierz Krajewski, "Walka 1 kompanii I/78 pp AK (Zgrupowanie Stołpeckie) z partyzantką sowiecką w Kamieniu (pow. Stołpce) nocą 14/15 maja 1944 r.," *ipn.gov.pl*, archived 11/06/2015 at the Wayback machine at https://web.archive.org/web/20151106190457/http://ipn.gov.pl/obep-warszawa/publikacje-internetowe-obep/walka-1-kompanii-i78-pp-ak-zgrupowanie-stolpeckie-z-partyzantka-sowiecka-w-ka (trans. from Polish).

- Marian Podgóreczny, *Zgrupowanie Stołpeckie–Nalibockie Armii Krajowej: Oszczerstwa i fakty. Wywiad z dowódcą Zgrupowania, cichociemnym, mjr Adolfem Pilchem ps. „Góra", „Dolina,"* (Sopot: Iwieniec.eu, 2010).

- Lukasz Zalesinski, "Bitwa o Kamień Stołpecki," *Polska Zbrojna*, May, 14, 2022 at https://polska-zbrojna.pl/Mobile/ArticleShow/37224 (trans. from Polish).

Józef's confrontation with Czech was told to the author by Paulina Nurt, and is also documented in:

- Stanisław Karlik, referencing a letter from Józef Jan Kuźmiński in "Bilans Powstania Iwienieckiego 19.06.1943 r.," *Kresy24.pl* at https://kresy24.pl/bilans-powstania-iwienieckiego/ (trans. from Polish).

- Józef Jan Kuźmiński, *Z Iwieńca i Stołpców* (Mireki, 2014)

- Marian Podgóreczny, *Doliniacy*, 2013 ed. (Mireki, 2013)

The high level of respect earned by Adolf Pilch from his soldiers is confirmed in almost all first-hand sources written by the men who followed his lead. This is also how Józef described Pilch, and so did the partisans whom the author spoke with or corresponded with.

For additional reading on Adolf Pilch, see:

- Kazimierz Krajewski, "Major Adolf Pilch „Góra", „Dolina" – dowódca Zgrupowania Stołpeckiego AK," *Instytut Pamięci Narodowej*, December 12, 2021 at https://przystanekhistoria.pl/pa2/teksty/88618,Major-Adolf-Pilch-Gora-Dolina-dowodca-Zgrupowania-Stolpeckiego-AK.html (trans. from Polish).

Regarding the lack of plans or help from Major Kalenkiewicz, he was severely injured in battle, on June 24,1944. He developed gangrene leading to amputation of his arm:

- "Major Maciej Kalenkiewicz (1906-1944), nom de guerre 'Kotwicz', And the Battle Against the NKVD At Surkonty - August 21, 1944," *Doomed Soldiers* at https://www.doomedsoldiers.com/maciej-kalenkiewicz-major.html.

Further reading on the SS RONA:

- "Grupa Kampinos: Działania bojowe," *Światowy Związek Żołnierzy Armii Krajowe* at https://ak-obroza-kampinos.waw.pl/44.html (trans. from Polish).

- Rolf Michaelis, *Russians in the Waffen-SS*, (United States: Schiffer Military History, 2009).

- "Rosyjska Narodowa Armia Wyzwoleńcza," *wilk.wpk.p.lodz.pl*, Archived 4/18/2008 at the Wayback Machine at https://web.archive.org/web/20080418091700/http://wilk.wpk.p.lodz.pl/~whatfor/rona.htm (trans. from Polish).

Chapter 19: The Trek -- Second Injury

The beginning of the chapter is drawn from Pilch's *Partyzanci Trzech Puszcz*, Podgóreczny's *Doliniaci*, and Józef's notes and stories.

The attack on July 1, 1944 is based on the author's interview with partisan Kazimierz Jankowski circa 2005, and is also referenced in:

- Szymon Nowak, *Puszcza Kampinoska-Jaktorów 1944* (Bellona, 2011).

- Marian Podgóreczny, *Doliniacy*, 2013 ed. (Mireki, 2013)

The next few paragraphs are drawn mainly from Pilch's *Partyzanci Trzech Puszcz* and Podgóreczny's *Doliniaci*.

The account of Józef's surgery, near amputation and recuperation is from Helena Niedzwiecka Filipek, with specific details from the November 1994 interview given to Larissa Niedzwiecka Doyle. Additional details were provided by Paulina Nurt and Kazimierz Jankowski.

Chapter 20: Journey to Warsaw, and Chapter 21: The Bridge

The information in these two chapters is drawn mainly from Pilch's *Partyzanci Trzech Puszcz*, Podgóreczny's *Dolianacy*, the documentary film "Partyzanci Trzech Puszcz" (TVP Historia, 2011), and interviews and correspondence with partisan Franciszek Kosowicz over a two year period, 2008-2009.

The crossing of the Vistula is well documented. Additional sources include:

- Kazimierz Krajewski and Tomasz Łabuszewski, eds. *Powstanie Warszawskie. Fakty i mity* (Warsaw, Instytut Pamięci Narodowej, 2006).

- Józef Jan Kuźmiński, *Z Iwieńca i Stołpców*, (Mireki, 2014).

Chapter 22: Kampinos Forest

The information in this chapter is drawn mainly from Józef's descriptions and:

- Jerzy Koszada, *Grupa Kampinos: Partyzanckie zgrupowanie Armii Krajowej* (Warsaw: ZP GRUPA, 2007).

- Józef Krzyczkowski, *Konspiracja i Powstanie w Kampinosie 1944* (Warsaw, Ludowa Spółdzielnia Wydawnicza, 1962)

- Adolph Pilch, *Partyzanci Trzech Puszcz* (Mireki, 2013)

- Marian Podgóreczny, *Doliniacy* (Mireki, 2013)

For additional reading see:

- Jerzy Misiak, "History of the Kampinos Forest," at https://archaeologyofmemory.files.wordpress.com/2016/02/jerzy-misiak_history-of-the-kampinos-forest.pdf

- Piotr Zawada, "Powstanie Warszawskie w Puszczy Kampinoskiej: Walki Grupy Kampinos w sierpniu i wrześniu 1944 roku," *Stowarzyszenie Odział Kawalerii Ochotniczej* at https://kawaleriaochotnicza.pl/2019/06/04/powstanie-warszawskie-w-puszczy-kampinoskiej-walki-grupy-kampinos-w-sierpniu-i-wrzesniu-1944-roku/ (trans. from Polish).

Chapter 23: The Free Republic

The main sources for this chapter are Podgóreczny's *Doliniaci*, Pilch's *Partyzanci Trzech Puszcz*, Koszada's *Grupa Kampinos*, and the articles under the heading "Kampinos Group" at the website https://ak-obroza-kampinos.waw.pl/index.html, especially the page on "Combat operations" (Działania bojowe) at https://ak-obroza-kampinos.waw.pl/44.html (trans. from Polish).

Paragraph 2 is based on Józef's descriptions and on the author's interviews with partisans Kazimierz Jankowski, Witold Grzybowski and Franciszek Kosowicz.

Józef's courier, "Sweet Tree" (słodkie drzewo) may have been Jan Szachnowski. According to an email from Witold Grzybowski in January of 2008, Szachnowski used that code name. However it is not certain. Sources list Szachnowski's birth year as 1919, the same as Józef's. In Józef's stories about the battle leading up to their capture by the Germans he called the courier "słodkie drzewo" but he always described him as a boy and gave the impression he was a teenager around 14 years old. In Józef's manuscript he also refers to the boy as "Frank."

For additional reading about the "Free Republic of Kampinos" see e.g.:

- Witold Grzybowski, *Spis żołnierzy Zgrupowania Stołpecko-Nalibockiego Armii Krajowej* (Warsaw: Witold Grzybowski, 2014).

- Kazimierz Krajewski and Tomasz Łabuszewski, eds. *Powstanie Warszawskie. Fakty i mity* (Warsaw, Instytut Pamięci Narodowej, 2006).

- Józef Krzyczkowski, *Konspiracja i powstanie w Kampinosie* (Warszawa, Ludowa Spółdzielnia Wydawnicza, 1962).

- Szymon Nowak, *Puszcza Kampinoska – Jaktorów 1944* (Warsaw, Bellona, 2011).

The passages about "Zagloba" and his adventure with the saber come from Józef's stories. "Zagloba" was the code name of partisan Henryk Żulis, and he died on September 29, 1944, however it is not known for sure if he was the boy with the saber in Józef's stories.

The German command's estimation that there were over twenty thousand Polish troops in Kampinos Forest is referenced in:

- Jerzy Koszada, *Grupa Kampinos: Partyzanckie zgrupowanie Armii Krajowej* (Warsaw: ZP GRUPA, 2007) p.87.

- Józef Krzyczkowski, *Konspiracja i powstanie w Kampinosie* (Warsaw, Ludowa Spółdzielnia Wydawnicza, 1962) p.319.

Chapter 24: Pochiecha

The main sources for this chapter were Podgóreczny's *Doliniaci*, Pilch's *Partyzanci Tzech Puszcz*, and Koszada's *Grupa Kampinos*.

The information in paragraphs 4-6 is mainly drawn from:

- Norman Davies, *Rising '44: The Battle for Warsaw* (New York: Penguin Books, 2005)

- Richard C. Lukas, ed., *Out of the Inferno: Poles Remember the Holocaust* (University Press of Kentucky, 2013)

The interview with Istvan Garami is written about in:

- Richard C. Lukas, ed., *Out of the Inferno: Poles Remember the Holocaust* (University Press of Kentucky, 2013) p.138

The original interview appeared in a 1968 Polish magazine, *Za Wolność i Lud*.

For more information on the female "Amazons," with mention of Helena Niedźwiecka see:

- "Kobiety – zasłużone amazonki 27. Pułku Ułanów AK im. Króla Stefana Batorego w konspiracji," *Stowarzyszenie Odział Kawalerii Ochotniczej* at https://kawaleriaochotnicza.pl/2019/06/02/kobiety-zasluzone-amazonki-27-pulku-ulanow-ak-im-krola-stefana-batorego-w-konspiracji/ (trans. from Polish).

There are a few mistakes in the article above, probably due to confusion between the roles of Helena Niedźwiecka and her sister Rufina Niedźwiecka. It is noted in the article that (translation from Polish):

> "During the trial of rtm. Zdzisław Nurkiewicz, [Helena Niedźwiecka] collected money and provided help to support the commander. In the times of the Polish People's Republic she was under surveillance."

This is most likely accurate of Rufina, not Helena. However the quote from Marian Podgóreczny mentioned in this article is certainly in reference to Helena:

> "... full of dedication, at every moment she was on the front line carrying out the wounded under machine gun fire at the risk of her own life".

Helena definitely carried out nursing duties in the 2nd squadron of the 27th Uhlan (Cavalry) Regiment, however it is not certain that Rufina did.

Chapter 25: Marianów

This chapter mainly draws upon Podgóreczny's *Doliniaci*, Pilch's *Partyzanci Trzech Puszcz*, and Józef's notes and stories.

According to Jerzy Koszada, the cavalry soldier who died in Marianów was Aleksander Kozioł "Bohun" from the 2nd squadron. However Józef Krzyczkowski, wrote that it was Aleksander Bohusz. See:

- Jerzy Koszada, *Grupa Kampinos: Partyzanckie zgrupowanie Armii Krajowej* (Warsaw: ZP GRUPA, 2007) p. 210.

- Józef Krzyczkowski, *Konspiracja I Powstanie w Kampinosie, 1944* (Warsaw: Ludowa Spółdzielnia Wydawnicza, 1962) p. 386

Chapter 26: The Bad and the Good

Most of this chapter is sourced from Podgóreczny's *Doliniaci*, Pilch's *Partyzanci Trzech Puszcz*, and Józef's notes.

Józef's notes outline visiting "my boys at Laski." It is known that Józef was in contact with Fr. Wyszyński, but it is not known exactly how or where he met him, so the scene of their meeting at the Laski hospital is artistic license.

For more reading on Cardinal Wyszyński, see:

- Andrzej Micewski, *Cardinal Wyszynski: A Biography* (Bookthrift Co., 1986)

- "Powstańcze Losy Księdza Stefana Wyszyńskiego," *Muzeum Jana Pawła II i Prymasa Wyszyńskiego*, at https://mt514.pl/powstancze-losy-ksiedza-porucznika-stefana-wyszynskiego/ (trans. from Polish).

The detail of the charred paper with "Thou shalt love" written on it is documented in many sources, especially:

- Stefan Wyszyński, *Droga życia* (Warsaw: Soli Deo, 2001).

Regarding General Vormann's concerns that the Red Army would link up with the Kampinos group, unbeknownst to Vormann, the Russians had no intention of linking with the Poles, but rather planned to allow them to be eliminated.

The rest of this chapter is derived from Józef's manuscript "The Changing Life of a Soldier" (part of his unfinished memoir *The Notebook of a Guerrilla Fighter*). Józef's final battles near Jaktorów and the events leading up to his capture by the Germans are the only fully written descriptions he completed, as opposed to his short notes and outlines referenced elsewhere. Additional details from this chapter are sourced from Podgóreczny's *Doliniaci* and Pilch's *Partyzanci Trzech Puszcz*.

Chapter 27: Jaktorów

This chapter is mainly derived from Józef's account "The Changing Life of a Soldier". Additional details were sourced from Podgóreczny's *Doliniaci*, Pilch's *Partyzanci Trzech Puszcz* and Koszada's *Grupa Kampinos*.

Chapter 28: Helena

From Helena's interview with Larissa Niedzwiecka Doyle, 1994

Acknowledgements

Many thanks are in order for those who worked so hard towards the completion of this book.

First of all is my wife Kathleen for her constant support, early editing, and good advice.

Danuta Knuth spent many hours translating the Polish books for me. There would be no book without her skill and talent.

My sister Larissa Doyle was one of the two main editors who helped catch typos as well as improving the overall language. Her hours of dedicated work were crucial.

Ben Knuth was an early reader who boosted me by positive feedback. As a history major, his advice and assistance with source citations was important.

My daughter Isabella Nurt for her talented involvement with the artwork and photos.

Andrew Gołębiowski has been a long time friend and has always helped me find Polish sources and contacts. Connecting me with author Sophie Hodorowicz Knab was a godsend, as she connected me to David Trawinski.

Stanislaw Plewako has been invaluable, not only for his wonderful web articles, but for also connecting me with soldiers from my father's squadron.

My brother in law, phenomenal artist Kenneth Doyle, provided the cover design.

My sister Renata Kraft and brother Richard Nurt, for support and recollections of my father's stories that escaped me. Renata was a final proofreader who contributed with edits and corrections, and my brother Richard Nurt also helped ensure historical accuracy. His incredible recall for our father's stories provided me with details that would otherwise have been lost.

And lastly, successful author David Trawinski, who arrived on the scene like the Polish cavalry charging down from the Kahlenberg at Vienna, to save the day when I was most discouraged. His offer to help shepherd the publishing process through, his incredible layout work, and his editing will never be forgotten by my family.

Addendum

Within days of finishing this book, John Roman Nurt came to the end of his four-year battle with cancer. As his brother Richard said, "Dad and Uncle Jan would have been so proud of you John. You fought this like a true soldier."

Rozkwitały pąki białych róż... just as Józef and Helena sang this song and remembered their brother Jan, we who are left behind have another Johnny to remember. We love you John.

www.ingramcontent.com/pod-product-compliance
Ingram Content Group UK Ltd.
Pitfield, Milton Keynes, MK11 3LW, UK
UKHW050907040625
6227UKWH00013B/23/J